Lesson Plans Using Graphic Organizers: Grade 3

Table of Contents

W9-DES-614

© Steck-Vaughn Company

Lesson Plans Using Graphic Organizers 3, SV 2071-0

Introduction

What is a good education? There are many different answers to that question and differences of opinions regarding what a good education is. One way that states decided to clarify this question was by developing educational standards. These standards detail what students should know and be able to do in each subject area at a given grade level. Standards are high and consistent expectations for all students.

Teachers use classroom activities and assessments to determine if students are meeting or exceeding established standards. With a heavy emphasis being placed on these assessments and the adoption of these standards, the focus of education becomes not just what teachers teach but also what students learn. Teachers must focus their classroom efforts on students' meeting and exceeding standards.

Because there is such strong emphasis placed on these standards and assessments, teachers are in need of lessons and graphic organizers that they can use to ensure that they are covering the standards. The purpose of this book is to provide detailed lessons in correlation to the standards listed in Steck-Vaughn's *Parents' Guide to Standards* (ISBN 0-8172-6184-2) using Madeline Hunter's model of anticipatory set, purpose, input, modeling, guided practice, check for understanding, independent practice, and closure. These steps provide an effective model for enhancing and maximizing learning:

- Anticipatory set: a short activity to focus the students' attention before the actual lesson begins
- Purpose: the reason the students need to learn this skill
- Input: the things the students need to be familiar with in order to understand the skill successfully (i.e., vocabulary words, concepts, etc.)
- Modeling: what the teacher shows in graphic form or what the finished product will look like
- Guided practice: the teacher leading students through the necessary steps to perform the skill
- Check for understanding: the teacher asking questions to determine if the students understand the skill and can apply it independently
- Independent practice: the students working independently applying the new skill
- Closure: working the wrap-up of the lesson

Each lesson consists of a lesson plan, a model, and reproducible practice and individual activities. Each lesson also contains a graphic organizer as a teaching and learning tool for each skill. These tools can be applied to other activities and are interchangeable across the curriculum. These lessons provide a resource to begin implementing the standards and ensuring students' mastery of these skills.

Organization

Each of the four units contains a variety of lessons and activities that correlate to specific standards for third grade in the areas of reading, math, science, and social studies.

- **Reading:** The lessons in the reading section are designed to address most of the standards for Language Arts. The activities provide graphic organizers and lessons that allow the students to read and understand a variety of materials, to predict and draw conclusions about stories, to use literary terminology, and to use comprehension strategies, such as comparing and contrasting, finding main idea, inferring, predicting, and summarizing. These lessons and activities can be modified to reach multiple intelligences.

- **Math:** The lessons in the math section are designed to address several of the math standards for third grade. They provide the opportunity for the students to construct, read, and interpret data, including tables, charts, and graphs. Students will use geometric concepts, properties, and relationships in problem-solving situations, and also practice the reasoning used in solving these problems.

- **Science:** In addressing the standards, these lessons allow the students to understand the purpose of scientific investigations, ask questions, state predictions, make observations, give reasonable explanations for data collected, use tables and charts to explain discoveries, and organize observations in written form.

- **Social Studies:** The lessons in this section are designed to address several standards for third-grade social studies. They encourage students to notice the cause and effect relationship of people with their environment, to use reference materials, and to sequence events in history.

Standards

This is a list of the standards adapted into the lesson plans and activities used, although not all of them are represented in this book.

Reading:
- Use comprehension strategies, with support including comparing and contrasting, developing awareness of text structure, finding main idea, inferring, predicting, and summarizing
- Select appropriate reading materials based on interest and readability
- Sequence events properly
- Begin to predict and draw conclusions about stories using context
- Begin to formulate questions about what students read, write, hear, and view
- Begin to use organizational skills, highlighting main idea
- Use literary terminology and begin to use plot

Math:
- Construct, use, and interpret tables, graphs, and charts to describe relationships and solve problems
- Construct, read, and interpret displays of data, including tables, charts, pictographs, and bar graphs
- Identify, sort, and classify solid geometric shapes

Science:
- Ask questions and state predictions (hypothesis) that can be addressed through scientific investigation, while in small groups
- Observe and give a reasonable explanation for data collected, while in small groups
- Use tables, pictures, and charts to explain in written form
- Organize observations through writing, drawing, and graphing
- Illustrate water cycles and life cycles in nature
- Categorize items into groups of natural objects and designed objects

Social Studies:
- Use charts or map keys to compare and contrast cultures: homes, industry, literature, food, crops, customs, clothing, music, jobs, school, art, and family
- Create simple time lines of historical events
- Use reference material to gather information

Dear Parent,

To ensure that your child has a successful year and meets the requirements to advance to the next grade, our district has developed standards that each child must master. I focus my lessons on those skills listed in each standard to make sure your child receives the proper instruction for those skills. During this school year, our class will be working with activities in reading, mathematics, science, and social studies. We will be completing activities that provide practice to ensure mastery of these important skills. You can play an active role in your child's education. There are many things that you can do to help your child gain a good education.

From time to time I may send home activity sheets. To help your child, please consider the following suggestions:

- Provide a quiet place for your child to study or do homework. Make sure your child has all the supplies necessary to complete the work.
- Set a time for your child to study or do homework. This will help your child manage his or her time better.
- Go over the activity's directions together. Make sure your child knows what he or she is supposed to do.
- Give help when needed, but remember that the activity is your child's responsibility.
- Check the activity when it is done. Go over any parts your child may have had trouble completing.
- Help your child study for tests by asking sample questions or going over the material to be covered.
- Review all of the work your child brings home, and note improvements as well as activities that need reviewing.

Together we can help your child maintain a positive attitude about the activities while ensuring academic growth and success. Let your child know that each activity provides an opportunity to have fun and to learn. Above all, enjoy this time you spend with your child. He or she will feel your support, and skills will improve with each activity's completion!

Thank you for your help!

Cordially,

List of Graphic Organizers

(Tool 1) Sequencing

Prepare: Copy page 8 for partners and pages 9 and 10 for each student. Gather clothes for anticipatory set. Make page 8 an overhead.

Anticipatory Set: Ask for a volunteer to put a T-shirt, sweater, and jacket on. After he or she puts it on, ask why it is important to put the T-shirt under the sweater. Have students give reasons explaining the importance of order.

Purpose: Explain that a new word for order is *sequence*. Say, "In today's lesson you will learn how to take events in a story and put them in order from beginning to end. Sequence is important, and without sequence, the story would not make sense."

Input: Define *sequence* as the order in which events occur.

Modeling: Read the sample passage. Ask a student to identify the first thing that happens in the story. Ask another student to identify the last thing to happen in the story. Then ask others to identify other events in the story. Using the graphic organizer on the bottom of that page, model how to fill in the first event and the last event.

Guided Practice: Explain to the students that they are going to work with partners to fill in the blank boxes with events that happen between the beginning and the end. They need to put them in the order in which they occur. Remind the students to use the passage to help them find the correct order. Monitor partners and use directive questions to help those students who need it.

Check for Understanding: After an appropriate amount of time, refocus the group to the overhead. Call on partners to provide answers to fill in the boxes. Ask them to explain why they think this event occurs next.

Independent Practice: After checking for understanding, pass out the new passage and blank graphic organizers. Explain that the students will work on their own to complete the graphic organizer using the new passage. Remind them to look for the first and last events before filling in the boxes. Monitor students as they work independently.

Closure: Review the definition of *sequence*. Ask students to review why sequence is important (e.g., getting dressed). Then have them list real world situations in which sequence is important.

A New Name

Little Deer was tired of his name. It was a name for a young boy. Now that Little Deer was ten summers old, he no longer thought he was a little boy. Little Deer knew he could not just change his name, so he talked to the elders of the tribe.

The elders of the tribe said Little Deer could earn a man's name by doing a brave deed. Little Deer could not think of a brave deed to do. Then one day Little Deer saw a wild horse charge toward his little sister. Without thinking of his own safety, Little Deer ran toward the horse, shouting and waving his arms. Just before the horse reached her, it turned away. The people of the tribe were so grateful to Little Deer that they changed his name to *Wild Horse*.

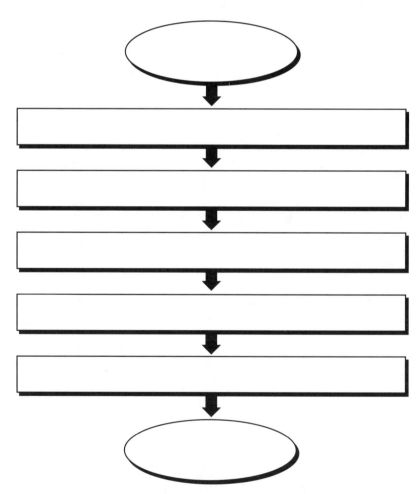

Snow Angel

Susan tied a wool scarf around her neck and put on her mittens. She opened the door, and a blast of cold air hit her face. Susan did not mind. She dragged her feet through knee-deep snow to the road and started walking slowly to school.

Susan blew and watched her breath form a cloud in the air. She looked around her and thought the snow sparkled like a million tiny diamonds. The morning was silent, and Susan felt peaceful as she walked down the road. Ahead of her, Susan saw two boys having a snowball fight. She did not want to be hit, so she turned to cut across the field behind the school. Once again she was walking in snow that reached her knees.

Suddenly, she fell face forward into the snow. Susan pushed herself up and looked down at the mark she had left in the snow. This gave her an idea. She turned around and fell backward in a clean, untouched area of snow. Then she opened and closed her arms and legs a few times. Carefully, Susan stood up without ruining her design. She had made an angel in the snow. Susan reached down and wrote: *Susan was here*. Then she brushed the snow off her coat and walked into the school.

Sequencing Flowchart

Title: _____

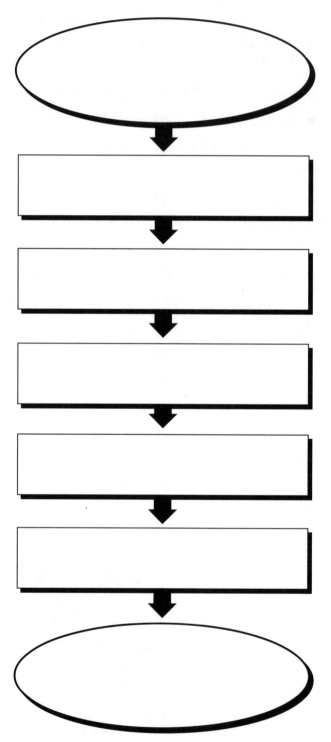

(Tool 2) Using a Story Map

Prepare: Make copies of page 12 for partners, make page 12 an overhead, and make copies of pages 13 and 14 for individual practice. Write five story elements and their definitions on sentence strips and put them in a pocket chart.

Anticipatory Set: Ask students to tell you things that every good story must have. When a student says a story element, turn its strip around. After students have mentioned each of the five story elements, ask them why these are important. Would a story make sense without characters? Without a setting?

Purpose: This lesson will help to identify the five story elements in a fiction story.

Input: Review the definition of *fiction*—a made-up or fantasy story—and the definitions of the five story elements: characters, setting, problem, events, and solution.

Modeling: Read the sample passage *Sweater Weather*. After reading, ask the students if the story has a character, setting, problem, or solution. Then fill in the characters in the story map as a class.

Guided Practice: Divide the class into groups to complete the rest of the story map. Remind them to review the story elements and look for those things in the passage. Monitor the groups, and use directive questions to have students discover the answers.

Check for Understanding: With the class as a whole group, ask for volunteers to complete the rest of the story map. Discuss how students identified the problem and solution. Why aren't these just events?

Independent Practice: Pass out the passage and new story map for independent work. Explain that the students will complete the chart using the passage. Review quickly the five story elements and their definitions. Monitor the students as they complete the map.

Closure: Review why the five story elements are important. Cover them up on the board, and have students volunteer to list and define the five story elements. Have the students choose a book for themselves and while reading, note the different story elements.

Name _____ Date _____

Sweater Weather

Once there was a kind woman named Mrs. McCan who lived all alone in a small cottage. The cottage had only a fireplace to heat it. Every winter Mrs. McCan bought wood for the fireplace and stayed nice and warm.

One winter there was no wood left to buy. Mrs. McCan did not know how she could stay warm. Mrs. McCan sat down to think about what she should do. While she thought, she began to knit a sweater. For many days Mrs. McCan sat and thought, knitting the entire time.

She stopped knitting one day and looked at the sweater. It was as big as the room.

"This is the answer!" Mrs. McCan said excitedly. She decided to knit a sweater for the cottage. Mrs. McCan measured the cottage and finished the sweater the next day.

To this day, every winter, Mrs. McCan wraps a large, warm sweater around the cottage. She stays warm and cozy all winter.

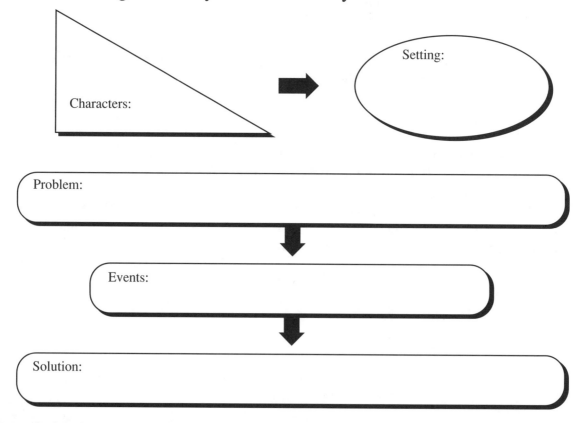

Name _____   Date _____

Emergency!

Kenny looked forward to Thanksgiving Day every year. His grandpa always came to visit. Grandpa would share stories with Kenny, and they would laugh and talk for hours.

One year, after the family had eaten their Thanksgiving meal, Kenny's parents and his brother went to see a movie. Kenny and his grandpa thought about what they could do during the afternoon.

"I know," Kenny said. "Let's play football! I need a lot of practice."

"That sounds like fun," answered Grandpa. "Find the football, and I'll meet you in the yard."

Kenny and Grandpa passed the football back and forth many times. They practiced passing and catching. Suddenly, as Grandpa reached to catch a pass, he fell down.

"Grandpa, what's wrong?" asked Kenny.

"I stepped in a hole and tripped, Kenny," Grandpa answered slowly. "I think I broke my ankle. You will need to call for help."

Kenny hurried into the house to make the call. Beside the telephone he saw a list of telephone numbers. He carefully dialed the number next to the word *emergency*. A man's voice answered at the other end. He asked Kenny several questions, and Kenny answered each one.

An ambulance and Kenny's parents arrived at almost the same time. Kenny could see that Grandpa was in good hands.

"We are glad that you were here to help Grandpa," Kenny's parents said. "We are proud of you for taking such good care of him."

Name_____ Date_____

Story Map

Title: _____

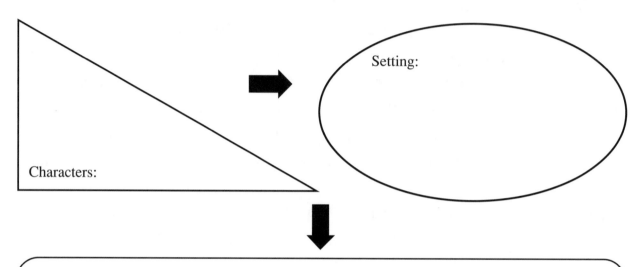

Characters:

Setting:

Problem:

Events:

Solution:

Tool 3 Predicting

Preparation: Write the five story elements and the probable passage words on sentence strips, cut them out, and put magnet tape on the back. Put the words in a pocket chart. Copy page 17 for partner work and pages 16 and 18 for independent practice. Make an overhead of page 18.

Anticipatory Set: Ask the students to help you think of the five story elements that every good story must have. As students say an element, have them define it and put it up on the board in this order: Character, Setting, Problem, Events, Solution.

Purpose: Explain that the lesson provides a review of story elements and practice predicting what a story will be about using story elements.

Input: Review the list of words. Familiarize students with the words, noting things such as if it is a name or a place or if it shows action.

Modeling: Explain that the students will categorize into five story elements these words from a story about which you have told them nothing. Model by using *Cameron*. The best place for *Cameron* would be under *Character* because it is a name, so place it in the *Character* column. Then choose a more difficult word like *fog* to model.

Guided Practice: Ask for one student to restate what it is they are to do with each word on their own paper. Then assign partners and give a time limit of fifteen minutes to complete the chart. Monitor and ask partners why they put certain words where they did.

Check for Understanding: On the class chart, call on partners to tell where they put each word and why. Emphasize that each group's chart may be different.

Independent Practice: Now explain that the next step will be to create a probable passage. Define *probable* as "probably," so the story will probably be right, or it will be close to the real story. Then, using the class chart, model how they will write their own probable passage on the overhead. Model how to fill in the blanks using each word in the columns to make complete sentences, and check them off. The students will go to their seats and complete their own probable passage. Monitor to make sure they are on task.

Closure: Refocus on the class chart. Review the five story elements and why they are important. Ask three students to share their probable passage with the class. After they have read, ask them if they want to know what the real story is about. Have them read it. Encourage them to note the differences between their passage and the real one. Invite the students to comment on how well they predicted the story.

The Lighthouse

As Cameron guided his boat among the rocks, he looked up occasionally at the old lighthouse on the bluff. He had heard stories about the place. They said that it still lit up on stormy nights although it had been empty for years. Even the old lens was gone. There was no way a light could shine from the house now. Most people stayed away from the place anyway. They thought it was creepy.

Cameron forgot about the lighthouse for a while. Then one day while he was out on his boat, a sudden fog moved in around him. He couldn't see a thing. He used his radio to call his dad.

"Stay where you are, son," said his father. "This fog will lift soon enough, and we'll get you out of there. I don't want you trying to move around those ledges now."

Cameron didn't like being fogged in. It made his skin crawl. He tried to relax. He was about to drop his anchor when he saw a light. It cut through the fog like a knife. Cameron couldn't believe his eyes. It was the lighthouse! For a moment, he wondered if it could be some kind of trick. What if the lighthouse had an evil spirit that would guide him right into the rocks? Cameron decided to trust the light. He started his engine and began to move slowly through the water.

Cameron made it home safely. His family didn't believe his story at first. But how else could he have gotten in past those rocks? Many people with more experience than Cameron had ended up wrecked in this kind of weather. Cameron knew just one thing for sure. He would never be afraid to go near the lighthouse again. Whatever was there had probably saved his life!

Probable Passage Words

bluff	boat	Cameron	lighthouse	radio
water	fog	rocks	father	scared
	move	light	saved	

CHARACTER

SETTING

PROBLEM

EVENTS

SOLUTION

Probable Passage

The characters in this story are _____

_____ .

The story takes place _____

_____ .

The problem in the story is _____

_____

_____

_____ .

Some things that happen in the story are _____

_____

_____

_____ .

The problem is solved when _____

_____

_____

_____ .

Tool 4 Stating the Plot

Prepare: Copy pages 20, 21, and 22 for students, and make page 20 an overhead.

Anticipatory Set: Ask how many of the students have ever missed the beginning of a good movie. Ask how that affects their understanding of the movie. Explain that stories are the same as movies in that they have a beginning, a middle, and an end.

Purpose: The reason it is important to be able to identify the story's beginning, middle, and end is to help understand the plot of the story.

Input: Define the *plot* as the point of the story and the story line. The beginning is the first part of the story. The end is the last part. The middle contains the important events that occur between the beginning and end—usually the problem.

Modeling: Place the page on the overhead. Read the first passage on page 20. Ask for students to tell what happened in the beginning of the story. Fill in the B/M/E chart as they answer. Explain that it is easier to identify the beginning and the end first. So ask for a student to identify the events at the end of the story. Then ask the students what was the most important part in the middle of the story. Hint—what was the problem?

Guided Practice: Divide the students into groups of three or four. Have them read the second passage. As a group, they should fill in the B/M/E chart. Monitor groups' work.

Check for Understanding: Refocus on the overhead. Ask for volunteers to give you the beginning, then the middle, then the end. Ask for reasons why they chose the events for the middle. Then ask what the story was about. This leads into the plot.

Independent Practice: Pass out the passage and B/M/E chart for individual work. Explain to the students that they will read the passage and use this passage to complete the chart. Monitor students as they work. Focus on the middle sections.

Closure: Ask students why it is important to have a beginning, a middle, and an end to a story. Ask them how they would feel if they were missing the last chapter of a really good book, or if the VCR tape broke in the middle of their favorite movie. Restate that you use the chart of B/M/E to help tell the plot of the story .

Practice: Stating the Plot

1. Carlos was finished decorating his holiday cards. He had bought the paper and stickers. He had cut out designs and glued them on the cards. He had written something special in each one. Then he had put stamps on the envelopes and mailed them. He could hardly wait until his friends and family opened them.

Beginning	Middle	End

2. Kim was so hungry! She had eaten very little all day. She had been late for school and ate only a piece of toast for breakfast. At lunch, she had been talking to her friends and ran out of time to finish her sandwich. Then she had to do some chores for Mrs. Brown on her way home from school, so she hadn't had a snack. Now her stomach was grumbling. She hurried to the kitchen to see what was for dinner.

Beginning	Middle	End

The Rocking Chair

One day when Beth walked by the nursery, she saw something very strange. The rocking chair was rocking, and no one was in the room! Beth thought that the wind must have made the chair rock, but the window was not open.

"Well," said Beth to herself, "there has to be some good explanation!"

The next day, though, the same thing happened. Beth began to think her house was haunted! She told her mother about it, but her mother just laughed.

"I'm sure there is a good reason why that chair was moving, Beth," she said. "Don't be concerned about it."

But Beth was worried—and spooked! How could she sleep near a haunted room? How could her mother put the baby in a haunted room?

Beth decided to hide and spy on the chair. She would catch the ghost in action! Beth hid behind the door and peered out the crack at the room. She was very nervous, but nothing happened for a long time. Then her cat came in the room. The cat was not allowed in the nursery, but Beth kept quiet. She did not want to give herself away. The cat got into the rocking chair. That annoying cat was going to ruin her investigation! She considered shooing away the naughty cat, but just then, her mother approached the doorway. The cat leapt from the chair and under the bed. The rocker rocked! It looked just as it had when Beth saw it. Beth laughed aloud. Now she knew what was haunting the nursery!

Beginning, Middle, and End

Read the passage. Complete the chart by writing what happened in the beginning, middle, and end of the story.

Beginning	Middle	End

Tool 5 Finding the Main Idea

Preparation: Make copies of pages 25 and 26. Make an overhead of page 24.

Anticipatory Set: Ask students to tell what their favorite movie is. Have them describe it in one sentence. Explain that they are telling you what the story is mostly about.

Purpose: Explain that they are going to find the main idea of several passages.

Input: Define *main idea* as what the story is mostly about. The sentences that support the main idea are called details.

Modeling: Place the passage about the goldfish on the overhead. Read it out loud, and ask your students if they can tell you what it is mostly about. Write that in the middle of the graphic organizer. Then ask what sentences support that main idea. Write them in the surrounding boxes. Repeat the process with the second paragraph.

Guided Practice: Divide the students into groups. Have them read the two paragraphs and use the graphic organizer to find the main ideas and details of the paragraphs. Monitor the students as they work.

Check for Understanding: Refocus the group and ask one student to volunteer to tell the main idea of the first paragraph. Then have the students explain which sentences are details. Repeat for the second paragraph. Have one student define the main idea.

Independent Practice: Pass out the page with graphic organizers and two paragraphs. Have the students read the paragraphs and complete the graphic organizers independently.

Closure: Review what the main idea and details are. Ask students how finding the main idea can be applied to real world situations.

www.svschoolsupply.com

© Steck-Vaughn Company

23

Unit One: Reading

Lesson Plans Using Graphic Organizers 3, SV 2071-0

Modeling Main Idea

My goldfish Sam likes to swim all the time. When I feed him, Sam swims to the top of his bowl. Sometimes, Sam swims from side to side. At night when I go to bed, Sam swims among the rocks at the bottom of his bowl.

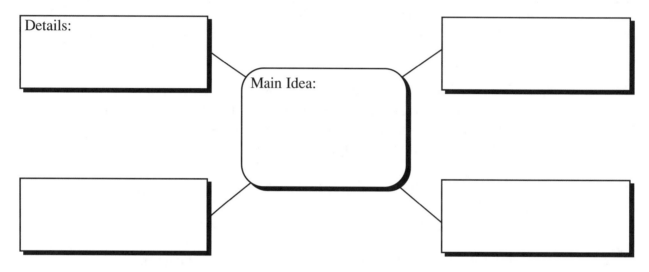

Details:

Main Idea:

Lana and her family were preparing for their summer vacation. They were going to the lake. They were packing the car. They packed clothes, books, and games for rainy days. Soon the car was full of their things.

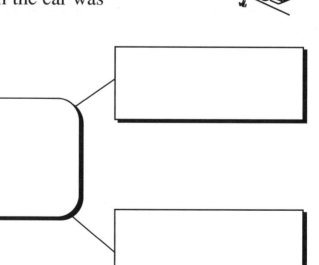

Details:

Main Idea:

Practice: Finding the Main Idea

1.   Janet decided it was time to plant her garden. She went to the garden shop and bought some seeds. She got her tools from the garage. She went to her garden spot and started breaking up the ground. She made rows and planted lettuce, onions, tomatoes, and green peppers.

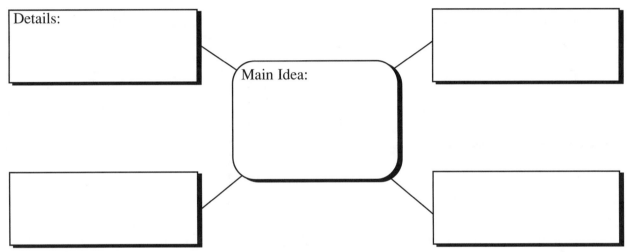

2.   It was a rainy Saturday afternoon. Karen and Gina decided to go to a movie. They got their raincoats and walked to the movie theater. They bought some popcorn and went in to enjoy the movie.

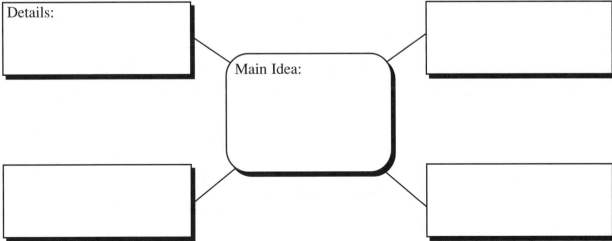

Finding the Main Idea

Identify the main idea and write it in the middle. Then write the details in the boxes.

1. Winter had come almost overnight. The new snow was just right for making a snowman. Sam put on his snow pants, coat, hat, and mittens. He got a carrot and some raisins. Sam went outside and began to roll the snow into large balls.

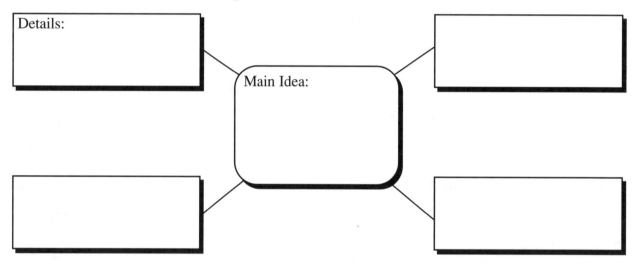

Details:

Main Idea:

2. The next day was very warm, and the snow began to melt. The snowman got smaller and smaller. First, his nose fell off. Then, his arms fell out. Finally, the snowman's body disappeared into a puddle of water.

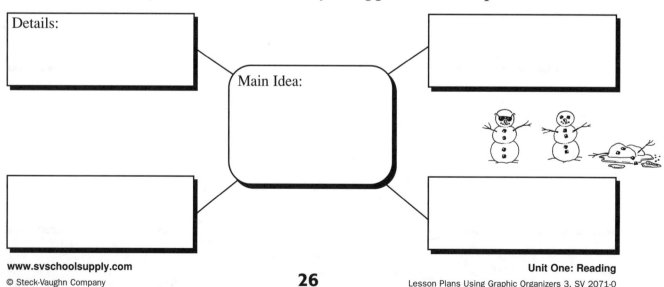

Details:

Main Idea:

Tool 6 Summarizing

Preparation: Make copies of pages 29 (two sets) and 30. Make an overhead of pages 28 and 29. Make the four letters *S*, *W*, *B*, and *S*, and put magnetic strips on them to attach them to the board.

Anticipatory Set: Put the four letters, *S*, *W*, *B*, and *S*, on the board. Ask students to predict what they stand for. Then, underneath each letter write: *S-somebody*, *W-wanted*, *B-but*, and *S-so*.

Purpose: Explain that the students are going to use these four letters to summarize a passage. The four letters are a part of a graphic organizer that will help them to summarize any story or passage.

Input: Define *summary* as highlighting the most important parts of the story or passage.

Modeling: Explain the model before you begin. Explain that the first *S* is the somebody or main character in the story. The *W* is what the main character wants to do in the story. The *B* is the "but" or the problem in the story. And the last *S* is the so or the solution to how the character works out the problem. Place the modeling passage on the overhead. Read the passage. Then put the model of SWBS on the overhead. Ask students to help you decide what to put under each column.

Guided Practice: Divide the students into groups. Then pass out the SWBS models for the students. Tell them not to complete the summary yet. Have them fill in the SWBS chart. Monitor the students as they work.

Check for Understanding: Review what SWBS stands for. Show the model on the overhead again. Ask for volunteers to help you complete it. Then model how they will use this to write the summary sentence at the bottom of the SWBS. Use the words under each column to complete the sentence.

Independent Practice: Pass out the pages with the SWBS graphic organizer and the reading passage. Have the students read the passage and complete the graphic organizer for this passage independently. Remind them how to complete the summary sentence. Monitor the students as they work.

Closure: Review what SWBS stands for. Ask students to repeat SWBS three times to commit it to memory. Then review what *S*, *W*, *B*, and *S* stand for. Ask students to think of other subjects or stories they can apply this model to for summarizing.

Name _____   Date _____

Just Plain Newton

Newton was a pig. He lived in a pigpen on a farm with many other
pigs. Newton looked like the other pigs he knew. This made Newton feel
plain and ordinary. Newton wanted to be special. He decided he needed to
act differently from the other pigs to be special. So, when the rest of the
pigs ate out of the trough, Newton put his food on a plate. When the other
pigs relaxed in the mud, Newton would not get himself dirty.

The other pigs did notice Newton, but not in the way that he wanted.
Instead of thinking Newton was special, the other pigs made fun of him.
They also stopped playing with him.

One day Newton realized acting differently did not make him special.
His friends had liked him before he started acting differently. So,
Newton went back to his old ways, and soon all the pigs were playing
with him again.

SWBS Graphic Organizer

Read the passage. Complete the chart. Use the information in the chart to write the summary.

S

(somebody)

W

(wanted)

B

(but)

S

(so)

Summary:

_____ wanted _____,

but _____

so _____.

The Candlemaker

There once was a candlemaker from Brighton who made wonderful candles of all colors, shapes, and sizes. People came from near and far to admire and buy his candles. The candlemaker enjoyed making his candles so much that it did not seem right to ask people to pay for them. He gave candles away until there was none left to give.

One day, he reached into his cupboard for more dye, and there was none. He searched for more tallow, and there was none. He found string for the wick. However, without tallow or dye he could not make any candles. He had given away his last candle, and he did not know what to do.

He went to see his friend the woodcutter.

"I have no candles to give to the people," he said. "You will need to work very hard to chop wood today. People will depend on the light from their fireplaces." It was soon known throughout the country that there were no more beautiful candles to be had in Brighton.

That evening, neighbors arrived with the woodcutter. They brought tallow and dye for the candlemaker. He was surprised and pleased. The candlemaker asked them why they had brought supplies.

"You have been giving us candles for years," answered the woodcutter. "Brighton would no longer be bright if you stopped making candles."

Tool 7 Identifying Cause and Effect

Prepare: Copy pages 33 and 34 for students. Make pages 32 and 33 an overhead.

Anticipatory Set: Turn off the lights in your room. Ask what happened. Then ask why it happened. Then explain that the lights went off because you flipped the switch. The switch was the cause for turning out the lights.

Purpose: Explain that things happen for a reason. There is a cause and an effect. Define *cause* and *effect,* and explain that you are going to apply cause and effect to the reading of a passage.

Input: Define *cause* as the reason why something happens and *effect* as what happens.

Modeling: Put the passage on the overhead. Read the passage with your students. Point to the graphic organizer for cause and effect. Review the definition of *cause* and of *effect*. State an effect, and have students tell the cause. Then state a cause, and have students tell the effect. Work together to complete the next passage and graphic organizer.

Guided Practice: Divide the students into pairs. Pass out the passage and graphic organizer of guided work. Have the students read the passage. They will work with their partners to complete the organizer.

Check for Understanding: Refocus on the overhead. Ask for volunteers to give you the effects and causes from the story. Ask students to define *cause* and *effect*.

Independent Practice: Pass out the passage and graphic organizer. Have the students read independently and fill in the causes and effects in the missing blanks. Monitor the students as they work.

Closure: Ask for a student to provide a real world example of a cause and an effect. Then have a student state an effect, and have another student suggest the cause. Ask for students to think about other subjects and situations that require the use of cause and effect.

Name _____   Date _____

Modeling Cause and Effect

Read this sentence and think about what happened.

The campfire went out because it started to rain.

The part of the sentence that tells "Why" is the *cause*. The part of the sentence that tells "What happened" is the *effect*.

Look at the sentence again.
    The campfire went out / because it started to rain.
        effect (what)   **cause** (why)

Read the story. Underline the effect, then answer the questions. Use complete sentences.

Harry won the bicycle race. He had been practicing every day. He was glad that his hard work had paid off!

Cause:		Effect:

Recognizing Cause and Effect

Write the effect and its cause for each sentence. Check your answers by asking, "What happened?" (the effect) and "Why did it happen?" (the cause).

1. Because Sheila ran, the dog chased her.

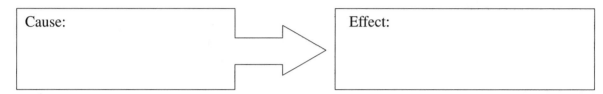

2. James dropped the ball because the Sun was in his eyes.

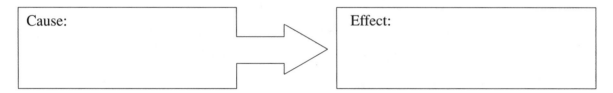

3. Since ladybugs eat harmful insects, gardeners like ladybugs.

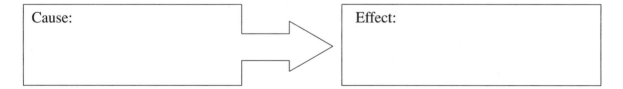

Cause and Effect Flowchart

Identify the cause for each effect. Some effects will have more than one cause.

1.   Amy was very sleepy. She had played basketball all afternoon. Amy fell asleep as soon as she got in bed.

Cause:		Effect:

2.   Robert went downtown. He wanted to buy his mother a birthday present. He also needed to buy a new softball. Robert was able to do both things in the same store.

Cause:		Effect:

3.   Tom's parents gave him a little extra money this week. Tom had done all his chores without being told. He had also cleaned the garage without his parents having to ask him. Tom decided to buy new handballs with his extra money.

Cause:		Effect:

Tool 8 Using Inference

Prepare: Copy pages 37 and 38 for students. Make page 36 an overhead. Wrap an empty box with wedding wrapping paper.

Anticipatory Set: Show your students a wrapped package in wedding paper. Ask students what they know about the package without seeing what is inside. Have them tell you things it could be and their reasons for choosing those things. Then have them say what it couldn't be and why.

Purpose: Tell your students that they use reasoning to infer things about the box. They apply what they know, what they are familiar with, and what they see. This is called inferring. Explain that the students can use inference to comprehend what they are reading.

Input: Define *inference* as a reading comprehension skill that lets you take what you know and put the facts together to figure something out without being told directly.

Modeling: Place the overhead sheet on the overhead. Read the first paragraph. Show students how you gather your information from what is given. Underline important information in the passage. Then model to your students how you would infer that Afi must have moved. Then look at your three answer choices and make the best choice. Then read the second paragraph. Ask students to help you identify things that you need to underline. Show them the three choices and have one student choose an answer. Repeat with the third passage.

Guided Practice: Divide students into partners and give them the practice sheet. Have them work with partners to choose the correct answers. Monitor the students as they work.

Check for Understanding: Have a student define *inference* for the class. Ask a student to tell which answer he or she chose for the first passage and why. Check the other two passages, and if students have different answers, have them explain their answers.

Independent Practice: Pass out the independent practice sheet. Have a student explain the process of finding the answer using inference. Monitor the students as they work independently.

Closure: Review the thought process of how students figure out what the wrapped box could be. Explain that we use inference to help us understand things all around us. Ask students to give examples of how they use inference in their own lives.

Modeling Inference

Use the information in each paragraph to figure out, or make an inference about, what the paragraph does not tell you. Put a check on the line by the correct answer.

1.　　　By the time the large truck pulled away, Afi was already unpacked. She looked around the strange new room. Then she looked out the window. Two girls just about her age were sitting on the porch next door. Afi hoped she would get to know them.

_____ Afi has been sent to her room as a punishment.

_____ Afi has switched rooms with her sister.

_____ Afi has moved into a new neighborhood.

2.　　　The engines roared as the ride began. Jennie leaned back in her seat and closed her eyes. A few minutes later, she looked out the window. Jennie leaned closer to the window and looked behind her. There, far away, was home—the planet Earth.

_____ Jennie is riding on a rocket ship.

_____ Jennie is riding a roller coaster.

_____ Jennie is riding on a train.

3.　　　Tran loved Jed, but he really hated this job. First, he had to get Jed to climb into the tub. When Jed was wet all over, Tran rubbed him with soap. Jed wiggled and tried to climb out of the tub. Tran tossed Jed a rubber toy, but that did not help. Jed jumped out and shook. Drops of water flew from Jed's furry body, and Tran was soaked. It happened every time.

_____ Jed is Tran's little brother.

_____ Jed is Tran's puppy.

_____ Jed is Tran's pet snake.

Practice: Using Inference

Read the story. Choose the phrase that best completes the sentence. Write its letter on the line.

1.   Angel Falls is a waterfall in Venezuela. Venezuela is a country in South America. Angel Falls is the highest waterfall in the world. It is a part of the Churún River. Its waters drop more than half a mile. Angel Falls was named after an American. His name was Jim Angel. He found the waterfall while hunting for gold.

_____ From this story you can tell
A. the Churún River is not very deep.
B. Angel Falls is found on a mountain.
C. Jim Angel found a gold mine.

2.   Do you like peanuts? Many people do. In fact, March is known as Peanut Month. People in the United States eat many peanuts. They eat more than one billion pounds of peanuts a year. Half of this is eaten as peanut butter.

_____ From this story you can tell
A. peanuts are a favorite American snack.
B. May is Peanut Month.
C. peanut butter is made from walnuts.

3.   The year was 1960. Chubby Checker was only 19 years old. Checker liked to dance. But he was tired of the same old dances. He wanted a new dance. So he made up a few new steps. The dance was called the Twist. He even wrote a song to go along with his new dance. Soon young people everywhere were doing the Twist.

_____ From this story you can tell.
A. people did not like Checker's new song.
B. Checker never learned to dance.
C. the Twist became a well-known dance.

Using Inference

Read the story. Choose the phrase that best completes the sentence. Write its letter on the line.

1.   Do you like pigs? Some people do. In fact, some people keep pigs as pets. Pigs are not really dirty animals. They really don't even smell bad. But they do like to roll around in the mud. This helps them keep cool. Did you know that pigs even have their own day? It's March 1, and it's called National Pig Day.

_____ From this story you can tell
A. pigs hate mud.
B. National Pig Day is in April.
C. pigs can make good pets.

2.   People once had to buy most of their food fresh. There were no frozen foods. Some foods were treated with salt to make them last longer. Vinegar was used to treat foods, too. Then in the 1920s, a man had an idea. His name was Charles Birdseye. His idea was to quick-freeze foods. His new idea was a success.

_____ From this story you can tell
A. salt freezes foods.
B. quick-freezing is a good way to store foods.
C. vinegar makes foods taste better.

3.   Every year people invent strange things. Sometimes these things are of some use. Many times they are not. Eyeglasses for chickens are an example. Chickens like to peck at each other. So someone made a pair of eyeglasses for chickens to wear. They were strapped on the birds' heads. They were meant to protect the chickens' eyes!

_____ From this story you can tell
A. the eyeglasses for chickens were of no use.
B. the eyeglasses helped the chickens read.
C. all chickens wear glasses today.

Tool 9 Using a Diagram

Prepare: Copy pages 41 and 42 for students. Make an overhead of page 40. Gather an apple, an orange, a banana, and some bottled water.

Anticipatory Set: Place an apple, a banana, an orange, and a bottle of water on a table. Ask the students how many different snacks they could have if they had to have one fruit and a drink. Have the students discuss the variety of combinations they could have. Ask if there is a way that they can show these combinations so they won't forget which ones they have already suggested.

Purpose: Suggest that the students use some type of diagram to help display their combinations visually. Tell them that diagrams are the tool that they will use to help solve some math problems today.

Input: Explain that a diagram is a graphic organizer that makes it easier to solve a problem.

Modeling: Show the diagram of the fruit problem on the overhead. Read the problem. Show how the list and lines help organize the information. Point to the fruit and drinks. Then show how the diagram makes it easy to solve the problem. Solve the problem by counting the different fruit and drink combinations.

Guided Practice: Review the steps to solve a problem with a diagram. Divide the students into partners. Give them the practice page. Read the directions together and talk through the process of having to complete a diagram using the information provided. Let the students complete the five problems with their partners. Monitor the students to check their progress.

Check for Understanding: Review the purpose of a diagram. Then go over the answers to the problem and creating the diagram. Check the answers. Realize that the answers may not be in the same order, but the combinations will be the same.

Independent Practice: Hand out the independent work. Read the information together and explain the activity where they will use the data to complete the diagram. Then look at problem number four. Explain that the students will have to create their own diagram that can be modeled after the one on the page. Monitor the students as they work individually.

Closure: Have students review the purpose of a diagram. Ask if anyone has ever used a diagram in a real world activity (In sports, diagrams are used to show winners and losers in a tournament.). There are many reasons to use a diagram in our daily lives.

Modeling Using a Diagram

Sometimes, putting information in a diagram makes it easier to solve a problem.

Read the problem.

For lunch, Iris can buy 1 apple, banana, orange, or pear. She can also buy milk, soda, juice, or hot chocolate. How many choices does Iris have for lunch?

Make a list of the choices.

Fruits	Drinks	Fruits

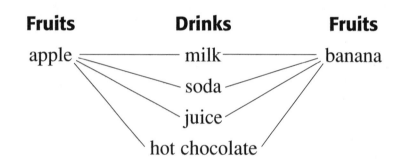

apple — milk — banana
soda
juice
hot chocolate

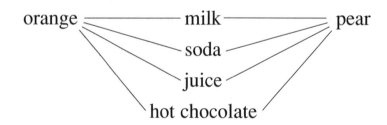

orange — milk — pear
soda
juice
hot chocolate

Solve the problem.

Iris can buy 4 different fruits.

She can buy 4 different drinks.

4 choices x 4 choices = 16. Iris has 16 different choices.

Practice: Using a Diagram

A **tree diagram** can help you list all the different combinations of a group of items.

David wants to buy a new bicycle. It can be 3-speed or 5-speed. It can be blue, red, yellow, or white.

Complete the tree diagram to see all of David's possible choices.

Speed	Color	Possibilities
	blue	3-speed, blue
3-speed	red	3-speed, red
	yellow	3-speed, yellow
	white	3-speed, white
	blue	**1.** _____
5-speed	red	**2.** _____
	yellow	**3.** _____
	white	**4.** _____

5. From how many types of bicycles can David choose? _____

6. Hyung went shopping for new clothes. He bought a plain shirt and a striped shirt. He bought brown pants, blue pants, and tan pants.

Complete the tree diagram to show all of the possible combinations.

Shirt	Pants	Possibilities
_____	_____	_____
	_____	_____
	_____	_____
_____	_____	_____
	_____	_____
	_____	_____

Name _____ Date _____

Using a Diagram to Solve a Problem

A restaurant offers the dinner menu shown here. You may choose one main course and one vegetable.

1. Complete the tree diagram to show all of your possible choices.

Main Course   **Vegetable** ⟶   **Possibilities**

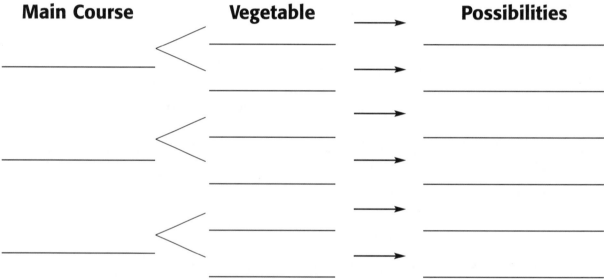

2. How many possible dinner choices are there? _____

3. The restaurant offers juice, water, or milk in small, medium, and large cups. Draw a tree diagram on a separate sheet of paper. How many beverage choices are there?

_____

4. The lunch menu includes tuna, peanut butter, beef, and egg sandwiches. With each sandwich, they serve a pear or an orange. Draw a tree diagram on a separate sheet of paper. How many lunch choices are there?

_____

Lesson Plans Using Graphic Organizers 3, SV 2071-0

Tool 10 Using a Chart

Preparation: Make copies of pages 45 and 46 for students. Make page 44 an overhead.

Anticipatory Set: Ask your students why we use charts. Let them list some reasons why charts are used.

Purpose: State that we are going to use charts to help us organize information. It is helpful to categorize and compile information in a chart to make comparisons and contrasts and to see the information in a clear order.

Input: Show the students a sample of a chart on page 44. Explain how to read a chart by looking at the rows and columns. Have them locate things on the chart orally to become familiar with the layout and purpose of a chart.

Modeling: Read the sample problem. Explain how this information would be easier to understand if it were in a chart. Show the chart and relate the information in the word problem to the information in the chart. Then show how to set up the equation using the chart.

Ann bought 9 yellow tulips, and Tom bought 7 yellow tulips.
So, how many more tulips did Anne buy?
$9 - 7 = 2$

Guided Practice: Review the purpose of using charts. Ask a student to give one reason why they are useful. Then pass out the activity sheet. Put students with partners, and have them complete the activities using charts. Monitor the students as they work, answering questions and guiding the students to complete the problems on their own.

Check for Understanding: Go over the problems with the whole group, asking for volunteers to work the problems on the board.

Independent Practice: After completing the sample problem, explain the directions for the independent activity. Tell the students that they will use the information in a word problem to complete a chart and answer questions. Pass out sheets for the students to work on independently. Monitor the students, and answer questions as needed.

Closure: Ask for volunteers to explain the skill learned in this lesson. Ask why charts are useful. Have the students list some real world experiences with charts.

Modeling a Chart

Sometimes, a problem has many facts. If you put the facts in a chart, you can see how the facts go together.

Read the problem.

Anne bought 1 white, 3 red, 9 yellow, and 5 purple tulips. Tom bought 2 white, 2 red, 7 yellow, and 10 purple tulips. Donna bought 8 white, 4 red, 1 yellow, and 6 purple tulips. Who bought more yellow tulips, Anne or Tom? How many more?

Make a chart.

	Anne	Tom	Donna
White tulips	1	2	8
Red tulips	3	2	4
Yellow tulips	9	7	1
Purple tulips	5	10	6

To solve the problem, read the chart.

Anne bought 9 yellow tulips. Tom bought 7 yellow tulips.

Then subtract to find the answer.

9 – 7 = 2

So, Anne bought 2 more yellow tulips than Tom bought.

1. Who bought more purple tulips, Tom or Donna?

_____

How many more?

_____

2. Donna bought how many more white tulips than Anne?

_____

Practice: Using Charts

Sometimes, a problem has many facts. If you put the facts in a chart, you can see how the facts go together.

Read the problem.

Carol bought 3 carrots, 4 onions, 6 squash, and 2 potatoes. Steve bought 5 carrots, 5 onions, 1 squash, and 6 potatoes. Jon bought 6 carrots, 3 onions, 3 squash, and 5 potatoes. Who bought more potatoes, Carol or Jon? How many more?

Make a chart.

	Carol	Steve	Jon
Carrots	3	5	6
Onions	4	5	3
Squash	6	1	3
Potatoes	2	6	5

To solve the problem, read the chart.

Carol bought 2 potatoes. Jon bought 5 potatoes.

Then subtract to find the answer.

5 − 2 = 3

So, Jon bought 3 more potatoes than Carol.

1. Who bought more squash, Steve or Carol?

_____

How many more?

_____

2. Steve bought how many more onions than Jon?

_____

Using a Chart to Solve a Problem

Sometimes, a problem has many facts. If you put the facts in a chart, you can see how the facts go together.

Read the problem.

Jenn bought 5 red, 4 yellow, 6 green, and 7 blue marbles. Jim bought 6 red, 2 yellow, 8 green, and 2 blue marbles. Kelly bought 6 red, 1 yellow, 10 green, and 4 blue marbles. Who bought more yellow marbles, Jenn or Jim? How many more?

Make a chart.

	Jenn	Jim	Kelly
Red			
Yellow			
Green			
Blue			

To solve the problem, read the chart.

Jenn bought _____ yellow marbles.   Jim bought _____ yellow marbles.

Write an equation: _____ − _____ = _____

So, _____ has _____ more yellow marbles than

_____ .

1. Who bought more green marbles, Jenn or Kelly?

   _____

2. How many more blue marbles did Kelly buy than Jim?

   _____

3. How many fewer red marbles does Jenn have than Jim?

   _____

4. How many more yellow marbles does Jenn have than Kelly?

   _____

Tool 11 Reading Line Graphs

Prepare: Copy pages 49 and 50 for students. Make an overhead of page 48.

Anticipatory Set: Show the picture of the line graph on the overhead. Ask students to tell you what they know just by looking at the graph. Ask why they might need to use a graph.

Purpose: Discuss the purpose of line graphs. Most line graphs are used to show changing data over a period of time. Ask the students if they can think of any data that may change over time (e.g., bank account, weight, temperature).

Input: Explain that the line graph has two points of reference. The left side is the scale, and it can be counted by multiples other than one. The bottom of the graph is the time period. This can also be counted in seconds, minutes, hours, days, weeks, months, or years.

Modeling: Show the graph on the overhead. Read the information shown on the line graph. Follow the line to each point, and ask the students what that point tells them. Then read questions 1–4, and work the problems together. Explain your thinking process out loud to model for the students how you interpret the graph and to make sure the students understand how to read the graph.

Guided Practice: Divide the students into partners. Give them the practice page. Read the directions together, and talk through the process. Let the students complete the four problems with their partners. Monitor the students to check their progress.

Check for Understanding: Review the purpose of a line graph. Check for those qualities in this graph. Then go over the answers to assess the students' progress.

Independent Practice: Hand out the independent work. Read the information together, and explain the activity where they will take the information and create the line graph. Monitor the students as they work individually.

Closure: Have students review the purpose of a line graph. Show the sample problem again on the overhead. Review how to read a line graph. Ask for any more examples of real world applications of a line graph.

Name _____   Date _____

Using Line Graphs

Line graphs are often used to show how data changes over time. This line graph shows the school attendance rate by month. To read it, put your finger on the bottom of the graph. Move your finger up to the dot for that month. Then move your finger to the left to find the percentage rate.

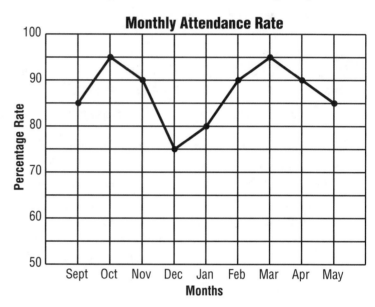

Use the graph to answer the questions below.

1. How much greater was attendance in September than in December?

_____

2. Attendance was how much greater in the highest month than in the lowest month?

_____

3. In what 3 months was the attendance rate the same?

_____

_____

4. Was the attendance rate higher in September–December or February–May?

_____

Lesson Plans Using Graphic Organizers 3, SV 2071-0

Practice: Using Line Graphs

The scale always runs along the left side of a line graph. The time period is set along the bottom of the graph.

This line graph shows the number of people who lived on farms in the United States.

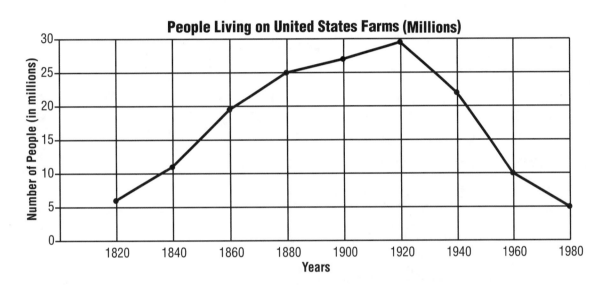

People Living on United States Farms (Millions)

Use the graph to answer the questions below.

1. In what year did the greatest number of people live on farms?

_____

2. During what 20-year period did the number of people living on farms increase the most?

_____

3. How many people lived on farms in 1980? In what year did about 5 times as many people live on farms?

_____

_____

4. Did the number of people living on farms increase or decrease between 1820 and 1900?

_____

_____

Line Graphs

The Fun Times Sporting Goods store made a line graph to show the number of sales for six months.

Fun Times Sales for Six Months

Use the graph to answer the questions below.

1. How many sales were made in November? _____

2. During which month was the number of sales the greatest? _____

3. In which months were the sales about the same? _____

_____

4. Make a line graph to show the average temperatures for October through March in Miami, Florida.

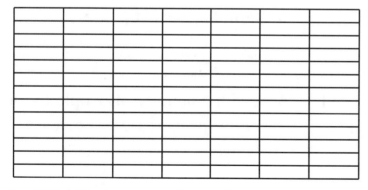

Temperatures in Miami, Florida

Month	Average Temperature
October	78°F
November	72°F
December	68°F
January	67°F
February	68°F
March	71°F

5. Which month had the highest temperature? _____

Tool 12 Using a Pictograph

Prepare: Copy pages 53 and 54 for students. Make an overhead of page 52.

Anticipatory Set: Show the Fido's Walk graph on the top half of the overhead. Ask students to tell you what they know just by looking at the graph. Ask what the pictures represent.

Purpose: Discuss the purpose of pictographs. Say, "We are going to use pictographs to help us solve math problems."

Input: Explain that a pictograph uses pictures to show information. It uses pictures to show data, and each picture stands for a certain number of people or things. Sometimes the picture stands for several or many things.

Modeling: Show the graph of Fido's Walk. Point to the names and the dogs. Point to the key that shows that one dog picture equals one walk. Read the questions and model how to use the graph to answer the questions. Then, show the second graph of Newspapers Sold. Ask students to note things about the graph. Ask how many newspapers each picture represents. Read the problem and the questions. Call on volunteers to help answer the questions.

Guided Practice: Divide the students into partners. Give them the practice page. Read the directions together, and talk through the process of having to complete a pictograph using the information provided. Let the students complete the five problems with their partners. Monitor the students to check progress.

Check for Understanding: Review the purpose of pictographs. Then go over the answers to the five problems and creating a pictograph. Make sure to focus on the key. Discuss what happens if the key is more or less than the given data (e.g., the key says the picture equals 5 but the data says 7).

Independent Practice: Hand out the independent work. Read the information together, and explain the activity where they will use the data, keys, and pictographs to solve problems 1–6. Monitor the students as they work individually.

Closure: Have students review the purpose of a pictograph. Show the sample problem again on the overhead. Review how to read a pictograph. Ask for any examples of real world applications of a pictograph.

For an extension activity, have the students make a pictograph. They can take a survey of their classmates and then compile their data into a pictograph. They can make a graph of eye color, hair color, favorite sport, food, animal, and more. Make sure they list a key and titles with their pictograph.

Using a Pictograph

Graphs are pictures showing information. A pictograph is one kind of graph. It uses pictures to show data. Each picture stands for a certain number of people or things.

Everyone in Felipe's family takes turns walking the dog. The family made a pictograph to show how many times each person walked the dog during 1 week. Use their pictograph to answer the questions below.

Fido's Walk

Dad	🐕 🐕 🐕 🐕 🐕 🐕
Mom	🐕 🐕 🐕 🐕 🐕
Felipe	🐕 🐕 🐕 🐕 🐕 🐕 🐕 🐕
Alma	🐕 🐕

🐕 = 1 walk

1. Who walked the dog the most times that week? _____

2. Who walked the dog 3 more times than Alma? _____

Dawn's father sells newspapers in his store. Dawn kept a list of the newspaper sales for 1 week. She made a pictograph for her father. Use her pictograph to answer the questions below. (Hint: Because each symbol stands for 5 copies, you can skip-count by fives.)

Newspapers Sold

The Sun	📰 📰 📰 📰 📰 📰 📰 📰
The News	📰 📰 📰
The Times	📰 📰 📰 📰 📰 📰

📰 = 5 copies of the newspaper

3. How many more copies of *The Sun* were sold than of *The Times*? _____

4. How many copies of all the newspapers were sold? _____

Name_____   Date _____

Practice: Reading Pictographs

A pictograph has a title and a picture key. The picture key tells what each picture stands for.

This pictograph shows the number of shirts a clothes store sells in 5 days.

Number of Shirts Sold

Monday	👕 👕 👕 👕 👕 👕
Tuesday	👕 👕 👕 👕
Wednesday	👕 👕
Thursday	👕 👕 👕 👕
Friday	👕 👕 👕 👕 👕 👕 👕 👕

👕 = 10 shirts

Use the pictograph to answer the questions below.

1. On which day were the fewest shirts sold? _____

2. Were more shirts sold on Tuesday or Wednesday? _____

3. How many shirts were sold on Wednesday? Friday? Monday?

The table shows the length of 4 canals. Use the information to make a pictograph.

Lengths of Four Canals

Canal	Length
Suez	100 miles
White Sea-Baltic	140 miles
Volga-Don	60 miles
Panama	50 miles

Lengths of Four Canals

Canal	Length
Suez	
White Sea-Baltic	
Volga-Don	
Panama	

≅ = 50 miles

Use your pictograph to answer the questions below.

4. Which canal is the longest? _____

5. How long is the Suez Canal? _____

Name_____   Date_____

Reading a Pictograph

**The pictograph shows the population in six United States cities.
Use the pictograph to answer the questions below.**

Population in Six United States Cities

Buffalo	⚐ ⚐ ⚐ ⚐		San Francisco	⚐ ⚐ ⚐ ⚐ ⚐ ⚐ ⚐
New Orleans	⚐ ⚐ ⚐ ⚐ ⚐ ⚐		Newark	⚐ ⚐ ⚐ ⚐
Baltimore	⚐ ⚐ ⚐ ⚐ ⚐ ⚐ ⚐ ⚐ ⚐		Phoenix	⚐ ⚐ ⚐ ⚐ ⚐ ⚐ ⚐ ⚐

⚐ = 100,000 people

1. About how many people live in San Francisco? _____

2. About how many more people live in Baltimore than Newark?

   _____

**Two music stores sell CDs. Use the pictographs to answer the
questions below.**

Melody Store

Kind of Music	CDs Sold
Pop	○ ○ ○ ○
Jazz	○ ○ ○ ○ ○ ○ ○
Classical	○ ○ ○ ○ ○

○ = 2 CDs

Music Barn

Kind of Music	CDs Sold
Pop	○ ○ ○ ○ ○ ○
Jazz	○ ○ ○
Rock	○ ○ ○ ○ ○ ○ ○ ○ ○

○ = 5 CDs

3. Which store sold rock music? How many rock CDs did it sell?

   _____

4. What kind of music did the Melody Store sell the most of?

   _____

5. Which store sold more jazz music? How many CDs did it sell?

   _____

6. How many more pop CDs did the Music Barn sell than the Melody Store?

   _____

Tool 13 Using a Table

Prepare: Copy pages 57 and 58 for students. Make an overhead of page 56.

Anticipatory Set: Show the picture of the table on the top half of the overhead. Ask students to tell you what they know just by looking at the table. Ask why they might need to use one of these.

Purpose: Discuss the purpose of tables. Explain that most tables are used to show information, or data, so the facts can easily be read or understood. Tell your students that they are going to use tables to help solve math problems.

Input: Explain that the table has information. Check the titles first, and check to see what kind of information is included in the table.

Modeling: Show the table of Monthly Kite Sales on the overhead. Read the information shown on the table. Then read questions 1 and 2, and work the problems together. Explain your thinking process out loud to model for the students how you interpret the graph and to make sure the students understand how to read the graph. Then look at the second table. Review looking at the title and information. Call on volunteers to help you solve problems 1–6.

Guided Practice: Divide the students into partners. Give them the practice page. Read the directions together, and talk through the process. Let the students complete the five problems and ordering the attendance figures from least to greatest with their partners. Monitor the students to check progress.

Check for Understanding: Review the purpose of a table. Check for those qualities in this table. Then go over the answers to the five problems and ordering to assess the students' progress.

Independent Practice: Hand out the independent work. Read the information together, and explain the activity where they will use the table to solve problems 1–5. Monitor the students as they work individually.

Closure: Have students review the purpose of a table. Show the sample problem again on the overhead. Review how to read a table. Ask for any examples of real world applications of a table.

Name_____   Date_____

Modeling Using Tables

Sometimes, a table gives several facts about one item. Carefully read the table to find the kinds of facts given.

The Kite Flight Store had a busy summer. They sold hundreds of kites. The table shows the kinds of kites and the number sold each month.

Monthly Kite Sales

	June	July	August
Butterfly	104	100	95
Dragon	52	62	72
Diamond	153	148	154
Streamer	140	160	129
Double Box	65	85	73

Use the table to answer the questions below.

1. Which kind of kite sold more units with each passing month?

_____

2. Which kind of kite sold fewer units with each passing month?

_____

The table shows below data about some tall buildings in the United States.

Tall Buildings in the United States

Building Name	Height in Feet
Sears Tower	1,454
Transamerica Pyramid	853
World Trade Center	1,377
United California Bank	858
Empire State Building	1,250

Use the table to answer the questions below.

3. How tall is the World Trade Center? _____

4. Which building is the shortest? _____

5. How much taller is the Sears Tower than the United California Bank?

_____

6. Which building is about 1,300 feet tall? _____

Name_____   Date _____

Practice: Using Tables

The list shows attendance at football games at a football stadium for 8 weeks.

Attendance at Stadium

Week 1	33,916	Week 5	28,246
Week 2	21,907	Week 6	19,886
Week 3	14,592	Week 7	31,991
Week 4	21,234	Week 8	44,045

Use the list to answer the questions below.

1. Make a table. Order the attendance figures from least to greatest.

Attendance	Week

2. In which week was the attendance the greatest? _____

3. In which week were the fewest people present? _____

4. In which weeks was attendance over 30,000? _____

5. Based on the information, what do you think attendance will be like in Week 9? Explain your reasoning. _____

_____

Using a Table to Solve a Problem

Be sure to identify what a question asks you to find. Then carefully check the facts in the table to find the correct information.

The table shows the pizzas sold at a pizza restaurant during the weekend.

Weekend Pizza Sales

Kind and Cost of Pizzas	Cheese $2.00	Sausage $4.00	Pepperoni $5.00
Saturday	40	32	55
Sunday	12	24	37
Totals			

Complete the table. Then use the table to answer the questions below.

1. How many sausage pizzas did the restaurant sell on both days? _____

2. On which day were the most pizzas sold? _____

3. Which pizzas cost the most? _____

4. How much would it cost to buy one of each kind of pizza? _____

5. How many and what kinds of pizzas could you buy for exactly $9.00? (Hint: There are 2 correct answers.) _____

_____

Tool 14 Counting Faces, Edges, and Vertices

Preparation: Make copies of pages 61 and 62 for students. Make an overhead of page 60.

Anticipatory Set: Ask students to review their flat shapes and their three-dimensional shapes. Point to objects in the room, and ask the students to identify their shape.

Purpose: Explain that these solid shapes have faces, edges, and vertices. The students are going to use the information about these solid shapes to complete a graphic organizer. This organizer will help them to compare shapes and note any relationships and patterns.

Input: Display the page of surfaces on the overhead. Define *faces* as the flat surface on a space figure, *edges* as the place where two faces meet, and *vertices* as the point where edges meet.

Modeling: Model how the students will count the faces by working the sample problems on the second half of the overhead. Ask the students to help you. Fill in the spaces for the number of faces.

Guided Practice: Divide the students in partners. Leave the overhead page on the overhead. Have the students complete page 61 with partners. Monitor the students.

Check for Understanding: Review the definitions of faces, edges, and vertices. Go over the page with the students, and have them explain how they got their answers.

Independent Practice: Explain that the students will now use the information they have on faces, edges, and vertices to complete a table. They will observe the shapes and fill in the number of faces, edges, and vertices for each. Pass out the table. Monitor the students as they work independently.

Closure: Review the definitions of faces, edges, and vertices. Ask the students to give real world examples of solid shapes, and have them tell how many faces, edges, and vertices those shapes have.

Identifying Surfaces

Cubes and rectangular prisms have flat surfaces.

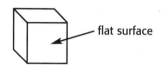

A sphere has a curved surface.

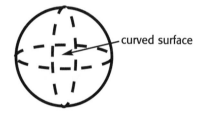

Cylinders and cones have both flat and curved surfaces.

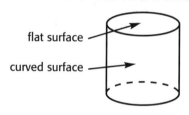
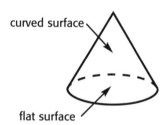

- Any flat surface of a space figure is called a **face**.
- An **edge** is where two faces meet.
- A **vertex** is where edges meet.
- This rectangular prism has 6 faces, 12 edges, and 8 vertices.

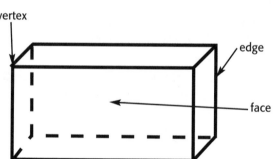

Write the number of surfaces.

1.

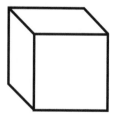

_____ flat

_____ curved

2.

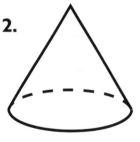

_____ flat

_____ curved

3.

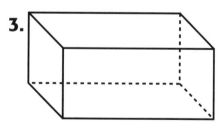

_____ flat

_____ curved

Name_____ Date _____

Identifying Faces, Edges, and Vertices

Write the number of surfaces.

1. 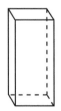 _____ flat
   _____ curved

2. 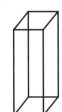 _____ flat
   _____ curved

Write the number of faces, edges, and vertices.

3. _____ faces
   _____ edges
   _____ vertices

4. _____ faces
   _____ edges
   _____ vertices

5. _____ faces
   _____ edges
   _____ vertices

6. _____ faces
   _____ edges
   _____ vertices

7. _____ faces
   _____ edges
   _____ vertices

8. _____ faces
   _____ edges
   _____ vertices

Counting Faces, Edges, and Vertices

| Cube | Cone | Cylinder | Sphere | Rectangular Prism | Pyramid |

Use the solid figures to complete the table.

Figure	Faces	Edges	Vertices
Cube			
Cone			
Cylinder			
Sphere			
Rectangular Prism			
Pyramid			

Tool 15   Predicting Outcomes Using the Scientific Method

Preparation: Gather one magnet, screw, plastic ruler, paper clips, washer, pencil, eraser, and penny for each pair of partners. Place the sets of objects at desks/stations prior to beginning the activity. Copy pages 65 and 66 for each student. Make an overhead of pages 64–66.

Anticipatory Set: Ask the students to look at the objects in front of them. Have them observe each object and then locate the magnet. Ask for volunteers to tell how a magnet can be used. Then read the passage about magnetism.

Purpose: The lesson today will be an experiment to discover what can be picked up by the magnetic field of a magnet. The students will use the scientific method to test a theory of magnetism.

Input: The scientific method consists of several steps: stating a problem, making the hypothesis, doing experimentation, making observations, and drawing a conclusion.

Modeling: Each student should have page 65 and page 66. Place the scientific method page on the overhead. Explain that the students will state the problem of the experiment. Ask for a student to state the problem. Then write it on the overhead. Then explain that the students will write a hypothesis for the experiment. They will predict what will be picked up by the magnets. Then show how they will complete the chart with a partner. Choose one object to model. First write the object, make a prediction, and test it.

Guided Practice: Have the students work with partners on problems 1-3. They will make a prediction first, then test their predictions. Monitor partners as they complete their charts.

Check for Understanding: Ask the students what they observed. Ask the students to tell how they tested their theories.

Independent Practice: Explain the rest of the activity. Explain the rest of the scientific model, and have the students complete page 66 independently. Have the students finish problems 4–8.

Closure: Ask for a student to restate the purpose of the experiment. Have a student restate the scientific method. Have the students predict what other things can be picked up by a magnet.

Magnetism

Magnets pick up and stick to many different things. They come in different shapes and sizes. They have different strengths, depending on their size. They have a force called a magnetic force. If not stored properly, magnets can lose their magnetic force.

Each end of a magnet is called a pole. There is a north pole, labeled *N*, and a south pole, labeled *S*. The magnetic force is strongest at the poles. The poles have different forces. If you put the ends of the poles of the two magnets close to each other, the magnets will either push away from each other or pull towards each other. If the magnets pull together, the poles are unlike poles. If they push apart, the poles are like poles.

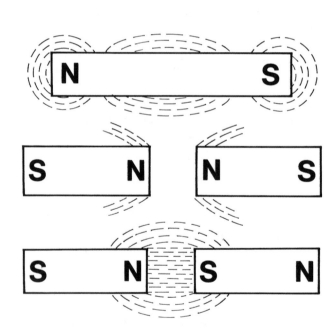

Scientific Method: Magnetism

The steps to help you solve a science problem are called the scientific method.

1. Problem: Identify a problem or question to investigate.

_____

_____

2. Hypothesis: Tell what you think the result will be of your experiment.

_____

_____

3. Experimentation: Will the magnet pick it up? Predict *yes* or *no*.

Object	Prediction	Result

Go on to the next page.

Scientific Method: Magnetism, p. 2

4. **Observations:** What do you notice about your experiment?

_____

_____

5. **Drawing a Conclusion:** Is your hypothesis correct?

_____

_____

_____

_____

Answer these questions using the chart.

6. Which objects stuck to the magnet? _____

7. What are these objects made of? _____

_____

8. Name three other objects that a magnet can pick up.

_____

_____

_____

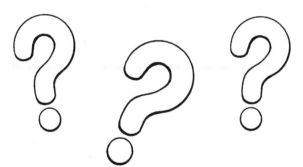

Tool 16 Using a KWL Chart

Preparation: Copy pages 69 and 70 for students. Make an overhead of page 68.

Anticipatory Set: Have the students observe the KWL chart. Have them predict what the *K, W,* and *L* stand for. Then explain that they will use this chart to help them understand a new concept.

Purpose: Explain that the KWL chart will help the students to organize what they know, to create a purpose for reading, and to discover the answers to their own questions.

Input: Explain that the *K* in the chart stands for "*Know,*" the *W* stands for "*Want to Know,*" and the *L* stands for "*Learned.*"

Modeling: Show the students the overhead page 68. Identify the topic, *comets*. Model how the students will complete a KWL chart. Start with *K*: ask what the students know about comets. Then have them identify the facts they know are true and the ones about which they are uncertain. Then for the *W* column, ask the students what they would like to know. Write their questions in this column. Then explain that you will now read the passage. As you read, answer any questions that the students asked in the *W* column. After reading, ask the students if you answered any of their questions. Then complete the *L* column with five things they learned from the passage.

Guided Practice: Explain that now the students are going to work on a KWL chart for another topic. Divide the students to work in partners. Pass out the KWL chart. Explain that the topic is *Planets*. Have the partners complete the *K* and *W* section for *Planets*.

Check for Understanding: Ask the students to state some of the things they know about planets. Then ask for some examples of questions they wrote in *Want to Know*. Have a student explain what they are to do with the *L* column. Then pass out the passage on planets.

Independent Practice: Have the students read independently. When they finish reading, have them complete the *L* column on their own.

Closure: Have the students review the purpose of the KWL chart. Ask them what the *K, W,* and *L* stand for. Then ask the students to tell what they learned about *planets*. Have them give examples of how they can apply this KWL chart to other things they do in school or at home.

Modeling KWL Charts

Topic: Comets

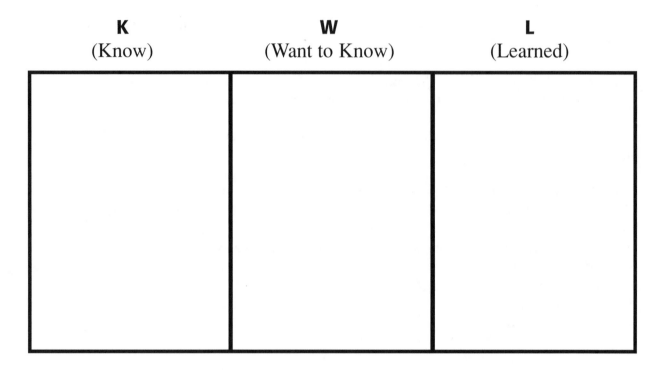

K (Know)	W (Want to Know)	L (Learned)

Comets

   Perhaps your students have heard of Halley's Comet. It makes an orbit near Earth about every 76 years. Comets are chunks of ice and rock that were left over when the solar system formed. Comets move around the Sun in oval-shaped orbits. Some comets take only three years to complete their orbits. Others take millions of years.

   The most unusual feature of a comet is its tail. As a comet nears the Sun, part of the comet begins to melt and turn to vapor. This process causes a long, visible gas tail to stream behind the comet. The tails of comets always point away from the Sun.

Name_____   Date_____

KWL Graphic Organizer

Topic: _____

K	W	L

The Planets

You know that the Earth is a planet. There are eight other planets near Earth. All nine planets travel around the Sun. Do you know what the word *planet* means? The people of long ago saw that some of the objects in the sky moved. They did not know what they were, They named them planets, which means wanderers.

The nine planets are all very different from each other. One reason is their distance from the Sun. Mercury is closest to the Sun. It is very hot there during the day. At night, it gets very cold. Pluto is the farthest from the Sun. It is sometimes covered with a layer of ice. At other times, it orbits close to the Sun. Then some of the ice melts. Venus is the second planet. Earth and Mars are next. Jupiter is the largest planet. It is the fifth planet from the Sun. Saturn, the sixth planet, is known for its rings. Uranus and Neptune are the seventh and eighth planets.

Our Earth is the third planet from the Sun. It is the only planet with life as we know it. This is because of our atmosphere. The atmosphere is a blanket of air. It surrounds Earth. It keeps Earth from getting too hot or too cold. It also keeps our water on the planet. The water allows everything to grow. We could not survive without it. Because of its life, Earth is a unique planet.

Tool 17   Understanding Cycles

Preparation: Make copies of pages 73 and 74 for students. Make an overhead of page 72.

Anticipatory Set: Draw a circle on the board. Ask the students what the word "cycle" means. Then ask if they can think of an example of a cycle.

Purpose: Explain that the purpose of today's lesson is to make students aware of the different cycles in the real world. There are many occurrences of cycles in nature.

Input: Define *cycle* as a process: the cycle begins at some point, goes through a process, and ends, only to repeat itself again.

Modeling: Place the overhead of the water cycle on the overhead projector. Read the passage that describes the water cycle. With the students' help, label the cycle in the picture. Then discuss how this cycle is relevant to the students' daily lives.

Guided Practice: Divide the students into partners. Explain that another type of cycle is a life cycle. Every living thing has a life cycle, so ask the students to list several examples. Read the directions and the passage pertaining to the life cycle of the butterfly. Have the partners work on the activity while monitoring their work.

Check for Understanding: Refocus the group, and ask for volunteers to tell the order in which they put their pictures. Ask the students to predict what the next steps would be.

Independent Practice: Review the definition of *cycle*. Explain that life cycles include plant life, also. Have the students complete the Life Cycle of a Plant activity.

Closure: Review the various cycles seen in this activity. Remind the students that cycles are a naturally occurring process. Have them think about the cycles in their lives.

Name _____ Date _____

The Water Cycle

Water often changes from its liquid form to its gaseous form. Then it can change back to its liquid form. This process is called the water cycle. There are three main steps in the water cycle. They are evaporation, condensation, and precipitation. Evaporation gets the liquid water into its gaseous form of water vapor in the air. Condensation turns the vapor back to a liquid in the clouds. And precipitation returns the liquid water to Earth.

Evaporation occurs as liquid water is heated and changed into water vapor. The water vapor is then carried up into the sky by rising air. Condensation takes place as the rising water vapor cools. The water vapor is changed into liquid water, forming clouds. Precipitation happens as water droplets grow heavy. They fall to Earth as rain, snow, or sleet. Water is constantly moving. It goes back and forth from the air to the ground in the water cycle.

Label the steps of the water cycle in the picture below. Write *evaporation*, *condensation*, or *precipitation* on the correct line.

Life Cycle of a Butterfly

Metamorphosis

The life cycles of some animals include a metamorphosis. A metamorphosis is a complete change in the animals. The butterfly goes through a cycle from a caterpillar to a butterfly. The egg hatches and develops into a caterpillar. The caterpillar eats leaves, grows, and develops. The caterpillar attaches itself to a tree and makes a pupa. Inside the pupa, the caterpillar is changing. After a short time, the caterpillar comes out of the pupa as a butterfly. It has changed through the process of metamorphosis.

With your partner, cut out the six squares. Number them and put them in order.

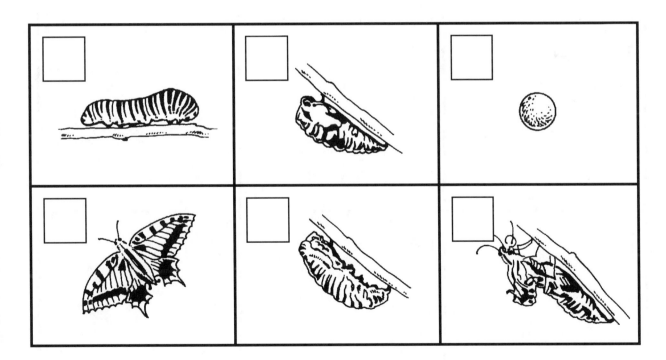

Name_____   Date _____

Life Cycle of a Plant

Living things have life cycles.

1. The life cycle of a plant begins with an embryo. An embryo comes from a fertilized egg. The egg cells of a seed plant develop in its flowers.
2. The seed sprouts.
3. A seedling grows.
4. The plant develops into an adult plant.
5. The adult plant produces flowers.
6. Inside the flower, new egg cells develop.

In the boxes below, draw pictures of the life cycle of a plant. You may use an encyclopedia to help you.

1.	2.	3.
4.	**5.**	**6.**

Tool 18 Classifying and Organizing

Preparation: Make copies of pages 76, 77, and 78. Make page 76 an overhead. Gather a shoe, sandal, tennis shoe, sock, pair of hose, a shirt, and a T-shirt.

Anticipatory Set: Have a shoe, sandal, tennis shoe, sock, pair of hose, shirt, and T-shirt on a table. Ask the students what all of these things are (articles of clothing). Then ask them if they can be divided into other categories. Show them that the shirts can go in one and the others are things to wear on your feet. Ask if the feet pile can be divided even further.

Purpose: Explain to your students that what you have done is called classifying and organizing. This is done in science to label animals, plants, and more.

Input: Explain to the students what it means to categorize—put in a group by similarities.

Modeling: Use the overhead of page 76 to show how to begin categorizing. Choose one article of clothing and put it into a category.

Guided Practice: Divide your students into partners. Explain the rest of the activity. Have the students complete the graphic organizer. Monitor the students as they work with their partners.

Check for Understanding: Have the students volunteer how they organized the first group. Ask why they chose to classify the way they did. Go over all of the possible answers, discussing the reasons behind each classification.

Independent Practice: Pass out the *Classifying and Organizing* page. Read the front with the students. Explain the activity. Have the students complete this activity independently.

Closure: Review with your students the purpose of classifying and organizing. Ask for examples of how classifying could be used in a real world situation.

Name _____   Date _____

Practice: Classifying and Organizing

Use the graphic organizer to classify the items below based on their traits.

jeans, tennis shoes, headband, jogging shoes, skirt, shorts, socks, hose, T-shirt, slacks, dress shirt, pants, tube socks, sandals, stockings, dress shoes, jacket, coat, hair clip

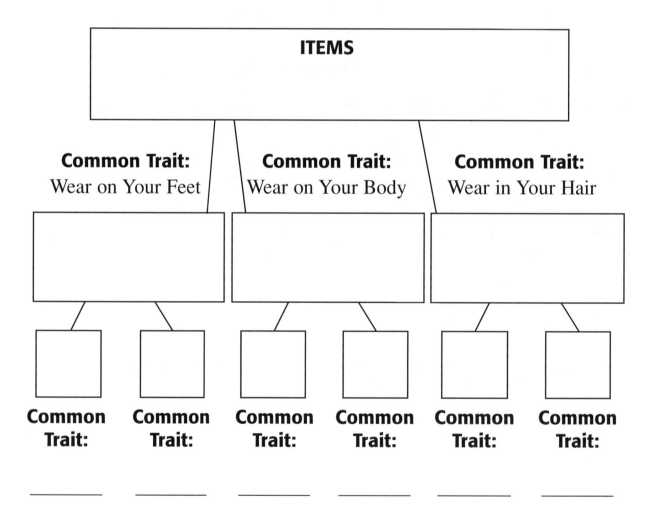

ITEMS

Common Trait:
Wear on Your Feet

Common Trait:
Wear on Your Body

Common Trait:
Wear in Your Hair

Common Trait:

Common Trait:

Common Trait:

Common Trait:

Common Trait:

Common Trait:

Classifying and Organizing

When you classify objects, you put them into groups according to how they are alike. Ordering is putting things into an order. For example, you might order things from first to last, smallest to biggest, or lightest to heaviest.

Think About Classifying/Ordering

Ask yourself:
1. What am I classifying?
2. What feature will I use to group my objects? Is there more than one way I can group my objects?
3. How does grouping my objects help me understand more about them?

Try It

The pictures below show different animals. The graphic organizer on the next page shows how the animals can be classified into three groups: those that live on land, those that live in water, and those that can live both on land and in water.

Go on to the next page.

Name_____   Date _____

Classifying and Organizing, p. 2

1.   Use the graphic organizer to classify the animals based on traits other than where they live. Think of a way to separate each group of animals into two additional groups. Write the names of the animals in the boxes. On the line under each box, write in the trait the animals in the box have in common. The first one has been started for you.

Animals
flamingo, parrot, tiger, dolphin, gecko, boa constrictor, guppy, shark, turtle, frog, wolf, water snake

Common Trait: Lives on Land

Common Trait: Lives in Water

Common Trait: Lives on Land and in Water

flamingo, parrot, tiger, gecko, wolf, boa constrictor	dolphin, guppy, shark	turtle, frog, water snake

tiger
wolf

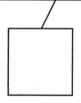 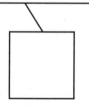 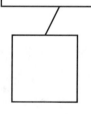 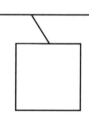

Common Trait:	**Common Trait:**	**Common Trait:**	**Common Trait:**	**Common Trait:**	**Common Trait:**
fur	_____	_____	_____	_____	_____

Reflect On The Process

2.   How did you use classifying to help you make choices about how animals can be grouped together?

_____

_____

Tool 19 Comparing and Contrasting

Preparation: Make copies of page 82 and two sets of page 81 for students. Make an overhead of pages 80 and 81. Gather a math and science book.

Anticipatory Set: Have the students look at a science book and a math book. Have them describe how the two books are similar. Then have them describe how they are different.

Purpose: Explain that what they are doing is comparing and contrasting. Tell students that comparing and contrasting help find the similarities and differences between two things.

Input: Define *comparing* as finding the similarities of two objects, and *contrasting* as finding the differences of two objects.

Modeling: Show students the example of a Venn diagram on the overhead. Explain that they are going to use this to compare and contrast Venus and Earth. Write *Venus* in one circle and *Earth* in the other. Then, explain that where the circles overlap they will list the similarities between the two. Read the passage. Then ask the students to find one thing that is similar between Venus and Earth. Write that in the middle. Then ask for one difference between Venus and Earth. Write the information about Venus in its circle and the information about Earth in its circle.

Guided Practice: Have the students divide into partners. Leave the passage on the overhead, and have partners choose three more differences and two more similarities. Monitor the partners working.

Check for Understanding: As a whole group, refocus the class. Ask for volunteers to share the similarities and differences they discovered. Ask how this information can help them when comparing and contrasting things.

Independent Practice: Review the Venn Diagram and its purpose. Then pass out the passage on *Tornadoes and Hurricanes*. Ask for a student to explain how to set up the Venn Diagram using the two topics. Then monitor the students as they complete the Venn Diagram independently.

Closure: Review what it means to compare and contrast. Then ask the students what they discovered when they compared and contrasted tornadoes and hurricanes. Ask for some examples of other things in their lives that they can compare and contrast.

Venus and Earth

For a long time, people thought of Venus as Earth's twin. They got this idea because Venus and Earth are about the same size. Venus turned out to be very different from Earth.

Venus has thick clouds. They are different from the clouds around Earth. The clouds of Venus are poisonous. They trap the Sun's heat.

There is no water on Venus. No plants grow. Much of Venus is quite flat. It has two areas of mountains. Its highest mountain is higher than any found on Earth.

 Mercury

 Venus

 Earth

 Mars

Name_____ Date _____

Comparing and Contrasting Venn Diagram

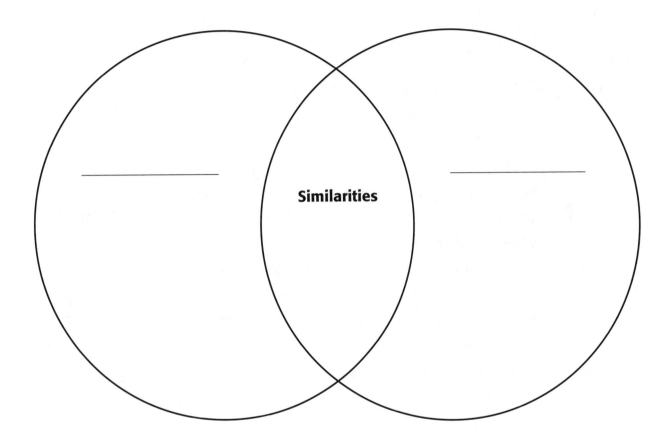

Similarities

Tornadoes and Hurricanes

A hurricane begins as a small thunderstorm over a warm tropical ocean. Then other thunderstorms begin to combine with it. The storms become a tropical storm. Soon the storm is moving westward, sucking in more air and spinning faster and faster. The storm becomes a hurricane when its winds reach 119 kilometers (75 miles per hour).

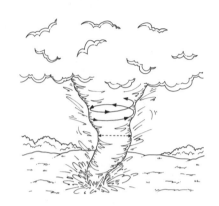

As it moves, the storm gains power. By the time the hurricane is a killer storm, its center, or eye, is much smaller—only about 50 kilometers (30 miles) across—and the air pressure inside the eye is very low. The hurricane has become dangerous. Buildings are turned into rubble, and boats are thrown into the air. Heavy rains can fall up to 5 centimeters per hour. Hurricanes cause more destruction every year than any other kind of storm. A hurricane can last from 4 to 14 days. As it moves inland, though, or over colder water, the hurricane slows down and eventually dies.

Tornadoes on the other hand, do not need a warm ocean over which to form. Many occur in the central states of the United States. Tornadoes do need thunderclouds, though. They also need warm air rising into the thunderclouds. As the warm air rises, the high winds of the thunderclouds start the air spinning. As the air spins, a funnel-shaped cloud starts forming close to the ground.

The funnel cloud itself is only a few dozen meters in diameter, and its center is usually only 100 meters (300 feet) wide. Tornadoes can last from 15 minutes to 5 hours. They can travel from 32 kilometers (20 miles) to 320 kilometers (200 miles) The air pressure inside the funnel cloud is much lower than outside, so the funnel sucks up everything in its path. It can take roofs off houses, lift animals high into the sky, and toss cars into the next block.

(Tool 20) Using Maps

Prepare: Copy pages 85 and 86 for students. Make page 84 an overhead.

Anticipatory Set: Have the students list the different reasons to use maps. List them on the board.

Purpose: Explain that the students will learn how to read various maps and understand their purpose.

Input: Define the parts of the maps you will show them. The first map is of the U.S., and it shows a compass rose and map key, or legend. Define *compass rose* as the tool to find the directions, and a *map key* shows what the symbols on the map represent.

Modeling: Put the map of the United States on the overhead. Walk through the different parts of the map, defining them as you go and showing examples. Read the questions, and show the students how to find the answers using the maps.

Guided Practice: Divide the students into groups. Have them work on another map. Review the purpose of the map key and compass rose. Monitor the students as they work.

Check for Understanding: Review the purpose of the map key and the compass rose. Ask the students to volunteer answers to the six questions. Check for understanding of how to use the map key and the compass rose. Review easy ways to remember the directions as Never Eat Sour Watermelons (N-E-S-W clockwise).

Independent Practice: Pass out the map for independent practice. Explain the directions. Explain that some maps show one kind of information. Remind the students to use the map key and the compass rose to answer the questions. Monitor the students as they work independently.

Closure: Review the parts of a map. Have the students define *map key* and its purpose and the *compass rose* and its function.

Using Map Keys and a Compass Rose

    A map is a drawing of a real place. All maps have a title to tell what the map shows. Symbols on the map stand for real things. To know what the symbols stand for, you will need to read the map key, or legend. Most maps also have a compass rose. The compass rose helps you find directions. It tells which direction is north (N), east (E), south (S), or west (W). These directions are called *cardinal directions*.

United States Map

Answer the questions.

1. What is the title of the map? _____

2. What does the compass rose tell you? _____

3. What does the star symbol in the legend mean? _____

4. Which state is east of Indiana? _____

5. Which country borders the United States to the south? _____

6. Which state touches land only on its northern border? _____

Name _____   Date _____

Reading Maps

A map's key uses pictures to show the location of special features, such as airports and bridges. The compass rose shows directions.

Study the map of the area of California near San Francisco. Use it to answer the questions.

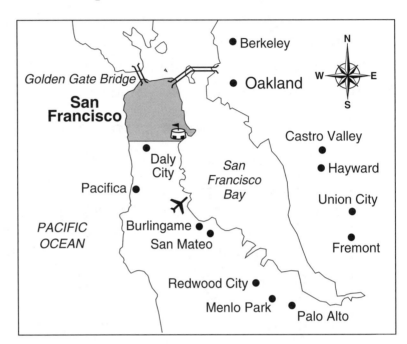

1. What ocean lies west of San Francisco? _____

2. What is the name of the bridge that leads directly north from San Francisco? _____

3. Could a person in a boat in San Francisco Bay see the ballpark?

   _____

4. What city is north of Oakland? _____

5. What symbol stands for the San Francisco airport? _____

6. Menlo Park lies between what two cities? _____
   and _____

Reading a Resource Map

Some maps show only one kind of information. A **population** map shows how many people live in different areas. A **precipitation** map shows how much rain or rain and snow an area gets each year. The map below is a **resource** map. This map shows where different kinds of trees and forests grow in the United States.

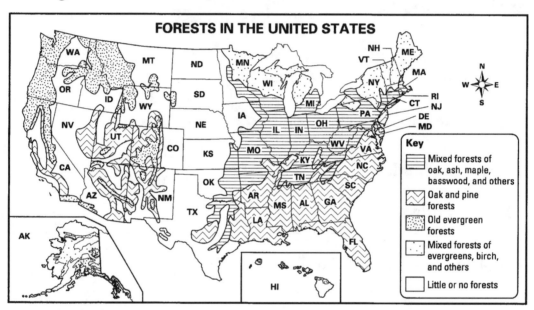

Answer the questions.

1. In which state would you find old evergreen forests?

_____

2. What kind of forest grows in the Northwest part of the United States?

_____

3. How many kinds of trees or forests are in Colorado? Name them.

_____

4. Find the state where you live. What kinds of trees or forests grow in your state?

_____

Tool 21 Using a Time Line

Prepare: Copy pages 89 and 90 for students. Make page 88 an overhead.
Write the dates of your birthday, first day of school, when you graduated from high school, when you graduated from college, and when you started teaching on sentence strips, and put them out of order in your pocket chart.

Anticipatory Set: Ask the students to observe the events in the pocket chart. Ask what they notice about the events (they have dates, they are out of order). Ask if the students can help you put them in order.

Purpose: Explain that events can be put in order on a time line. Explain that the students will learn how to read time lines, recognize the variety of time lines, and complete a time line using information.

Input: Define a *time line* as a graphic organizer that shows the sequence of events based on time.

Modeling: Put the time line on the overhead. Read the time line with the students. Help them read the time line by pointing out the format and sequence. Then read the questions on the bottom of the page, and ask the students to answer them orally.

Guided Practice: Divide the students into partners. Pass out the time line and graphic organizer. Have them read the passage and use the information in the passage to complete the time line. Monitor their work.

Check for Understanding: Reread the passage as a whole group. Ask for volunteers to supply the information to complete the time line. Review the purpose of a time line and compare the dates used in this outline versus the one on the overhead (years versus months).

Independent Practice: Pass out the passage and graphic organizer. Have the students read independently and fill in the time line using the information gathered from the passage. Monitor the students as they work.

Closure: Review the formats and purpose of a time line. Look back at your pocket chart, and ask if there were other ways to show these events in order. Invite the students to create a time line of their own lives.

Name_____ Date _____

Modeling How to Use a Time Line

Examine the time line. A third-grade class has planned to do a play. Here is how they organized the events.

April 3	Class selects play to be performed.
April 4	Copies of the play handed out.
April 6	Tryouts begin.
April 7	Parts assigned.
April 9	Committees formed for advertising, props, tickets and programs, and costumes.
April 12	Rehearsals begin. Costumes fitted.
April 22	Advertising posters set up.
April 23	Tickets go on sale.
April 26	Costumes completed. Props completed.
May 1	Dress rehearsal (other classrooms invited).
May 2	Performance (family and friends).

Read each statement. Mark each *T* (true) or *F* (false).

_____ **1.** Tryouts for the play were April 9th and 10th.

_____ **2.** The advertising committee was formed after the parts were assigned.

_____ **3.** Other school classes were invited to attend the dress rehearsal.

_____ **4.** The costume fittings were the same day as rehearsals began.

Reading a Time Line

Examine this time line.

1980 —	John Crane was born.
1981 —	John took his first steps.
1983 —	John started nursery school; a sister, Anna, was born.
1986 —	John began first grade.

A time line is a kind of chart that shows the dates when different events happened. Events are listed in chronological order, the order in which they occur. Dates and descriptions are part of a time line.

Read this paragraph. Create a time line by matching the underlined events to the dates when they took place on a time line.

Daniel Boone is an American hero. He was born near Reading, Pennsylvania, in 1734. When he was 16 years old, he moved with his family to North Carolina. Daniel was a true pioneer, eager to explore new lands and meet new challenges. He took part in the French and Indian War in 1755. At the age of 22, he married Rebecca Ryan.

1. 1734 _____

2. 1750 _____

3. 1755 _____

4. 1756 _____

Creating a Time Line

Read the story. Mark the time line to show when each event happened.

Keeping in touch with loved ones was hard for early settlers in the United States. In the early 1600s, people left letters at inns in seaports and hoped someone would take them to Europe. Between 1672 and 1763, governors in the colonies began planning mail routes. In 1789, the *Constitution* made the post office official.

That was fine for people who lived in the colonies. Private mail carriers served the settlers who moved west in the mid-1800s. One carrier was the Pony Express. By 1869, the railroad stretched across the country.

As the United States became more settled, the postal service grew. In 1963, a big change came to the whole country. Every address got a ZIP code. ZIP codes made it possible to begin using machines to sort mail.

In recent times, mail delivery has changed most of all. Electronics is the reason for the change. By the early 1990s, people had begun to use fax machines and computer mail, or e-mail. Now mail can be sent instantly. What do you think will happen in the future?

1600s	1700s	1800s	1900s	2000s

4. _____

7. _____

8. _____

2. _____

3. _____

1. _____

6. _____

5. _____

(Tool 22) Using the Dictionary

Prepare: Copy pages 93 and 94 for practice. Make page 92 an overhead. Gather a few dictionaries.

Anticipatory Set: Write the word *cape* on the board. Ask the students where they can find out what that word means. After you hear several different answers, show your dictionary, and ask if it can help. Then ask if they know what other information they can find in a dictionary.

Purpose: Explain that you will be using a dictionary to find out many different things about words, looking at how a dictionary is set up, and where to look to find information.

Input: Open the dictionary to any page and show students the guide words at the top of each page, the entry words, the symbols for syllables, pronunciation, and parts of speech, and the definitions.

Modeling: Put the dictionary excerpt on the overhead. Read the definitions, and point to the example. Ask the students to locate the guide words, the entry word, the part of speech, the pronunciation, and the definitions. Answer the questions with the students on the bottom of the page.

Guided Practice: Divide the students into partners. Review that the words in the dictionary are in alphabetical order. Explain the directions, and orally work the first problem. Then monitor the partners as they complete the sheet.

Check for Understanding: Review the format of a dictionary. Then go over the answers to page 93. Ask the students to tell you which word they crossed out, and then have them tell you which words go in each box. Check to make sure that they understand the concept of guide words.

Independent Practice: Pass out the work for independent practice. Explain the directions, and monitor the students as they work.

Closure: Review the parts of a dictionary. Ask for volunteers to use the dictionary to look up words, find its guide words, its part of speech, pronunciation, and definitions.

Dictionary Skills

- The order of letters from A to Z is called **alphabetical order**. Words in a dictionary are listed in alphabetical order.

- There are two **guide words** at the top of every dictionary page. The word on the left is the first word on the page. The word on the right is the last word. All the other words on the page are in alphabetical order between the guide words.

- Each word in the dictionary is an **entry word**.

- A **syllable** is a word part that has only one vowel sound. Each entry word in the dictionary is divided into syllables.

- A **pronunciation** follows each entry word. It shows how to say the word. It also shows the number of syllables in the word.

> **phlox [floks]   spinach [spin′ich]**

Use the example dictionary page to answer these questions.

> **cherry**   **chip**
>
> **cher·ry** [cher′ē] *n., pl.* **cher·ries**   **child** [chīld] *n., pl.* **chil·dren**
>   1 A small, round, eatable fruit, red,   [chil′dren] 1 A baby. 2 A young
>   yellow, or nearly black in color, and   boy or girl. 3 A son or daughter.
>   having a single pit. 2 The tree   4 A person from a certain family.
>   bearing this fruit. 3 The wood of
>   this tree. 4 A bright red color.

1. What is the last word on this page? _____

How do you know? _____

2. Which of these words would come before *cherry* in the dictionary?

> *carrot*, *corn*, *cactus*, and *clover* _____

3. Would the word *chop* be on this page? _____

Name _____   Date _____

Using Guide Words

Guide words at the top of a dictionary page help you find words quickly. The word on the left is the first word on the page. The word on the right is the last word.

Look at the guide words. Then read the entry words. Cross out the entry words that do not belong on the page.

1. blur 63 boat	**2. knight 95 koala**	**3. yard 225 young**
boat	knit	yourself
blush	kit	yellow
boil	kung fu	yesterday
board	knowledge	yak

Write the words from the box below on the correct dictionary page.

icicle	journal	hydrogen	kind	isn't
jacket	key	human	jeep	junk
kettle	idea	just	ivy	howl

4. housefly iris	**5. iron jumbo**	**6. jump kit**
_____	_____	_____
_____	_____	_____
_____	_____	_____
_____	_____	_____
_____	_____	_____

Name _____   Date _____

Using a Dictionary

- An **entry** is all the information about an entry word.

- A **definition** is the meaning of a word. Many words have more than one definition. Each definition is numbered.

- A definition is often followed by an **example** that shows how to use the word.

---

spin [spin] *v.* **1** To draw out and twist (as cotton or flax) into thread. **2** To make fibers into (threads or yarn) by spinning. **3** To make something, as a web or cocoon, from sticky fibers from an insect's body: Wolf spiders do not *spin* webs. **4** To turn or whirl about; rotate: to *spin* a top. **5** To make up a story or tale.

Use the entry for *spin* to answer the following questions.

1. How many definitions are given for the entry word? _____

2. For which definition is there an example sentence?

_____

3. How many syllables does the entry word have? _____

4. What information is given in brackets? [ ] _____

5. Which definition of *spin* is used in this sentence?
Rumpelstiltskin could *spin* straw into gold.

_____

Answer Key

p. 10   (IP) Susan started walking to school., She saw two boys having a snowball fight., She took a shortcut., The snow was deep, and she fell., She made a snow angel., She wrote: *Susan was here.*, She walked to school.

p. 12   (GP) Characters: Mrs. McCan; Setting: Mrs. McCan's house.; Problem: There was no wood for Mrs. McCan to stay warm.; Events: She began to knit a sweater., The sweater got bigger.; Solution: Mrs. McCan wrapped the sweater around the house.

p. 14   (IP) Characters: Kenny, Grandpa, Kenny's parents and brother; Setting: yard, house; Problem: Grandpa tripped and hurt his ankle. Events: Kenny and Grandpa played football; Kenny called an ambulance to help Grandpa. Solution: Grandpa would be okay.

p. 17,18   Answers will vary.

p. 20   (GP) 1. B: He bought the things to make the cards, M: He made the cards, E: He could hardly wait to have his friends and family open them; 2. B: Kim was late for school so she only ate toast, M: She was talking and didn't finish her lunch, E: She hurried to see what was for dinner.

p. 22   (IP) B: Beth saw the rocking chair rocking, but no one was in it.; M: Beth decided to hide and spy on the chair in the nursery.; E: Beth discovered that it was her cat leaping off the chair that made it rock.

p. 24   First passage – Main idea: My goldfish Sam likes to swim all the time. Details: all other sentences. Second passage – Main idea: Lana and her family were preparing for their summer vacation. Details: all other sentences.

p. 25   (GP)1. Main Idea: Janet decided it was time to plant her garden. Details: she bought seeds; she got her tools; she started breaking the ground; she planted lettuce, onions, tomatoes, and green peppers. 2. Main Idea: Karen and Gina decided to go to a movie. Details: it was raining; they walked to the movies; they bought popcorn; the went in to enjoy the movie.

p. 26   (IP) 1. Main Idea: Sam made a snowman. Details: the snow was right for making a snowman; Sam got dressed; he got a carrot and some raisins; Sam rolled the snow into large balls. 2. Main Idea: The snow began to melt. Details: the snowman got smaller; his nose fell off; his arms fell out; his body disappeared into a puddle.

p. 29   (GP) S: Newton, W: to be special, B: the other pigs made fun of him, S: Newton went back to his old ways. Summary: Newton wanted to be special, but the other pigs made fun of him, so Newton went back to his old ways.

p. 30   (IP) S: The Candlemaker, W: to give candles away, B: he ran out of dye and tallow, S: the neighbors brought him the supplies. Summary: The Candlemaker wanted to give candles away, but he ran out of dye and tallow, so the neighbors brought him the supplies.

p. 32   Cause: He had been practicing every day. Effect: Harry won the bicycle race.

p. 33   (GP) 1. C: Sheila ran, E: the dog chased her; 2. C: the Sun was in his eyes, E: James dropped the ball; 3. C: ladybugs eat harmful insects, E: gardeners like ladybugs.

p. 34   (IP) 1. C: She had played basketball all afternoon, E: Amy was sleepy; 2. C: He wanted to buy his mother a birthday present, E: Robert went downtown, C: He also needed to buy a new softball, E: Robert went downtown; 3. C: Tom had done all of his chores, E: Tom's parents gave him extra money, C: He cleaned the garage, E: Tom's parents gave him extra money.

p. 36   1. Afi has moved into a new neighborhood. 2. Jennie is riding on a rocket ship. 3. Jed is Tran's puppy.

p. 37   (GP) 1. B, 2. A, 3. C

p. 38   (IP) 1. C, 2. B, 3. A

p. 41   1. 5-speed, blue 2. 5-speed, red 3. 5-speed, yellow 4. 5-speed, white 5. 8 6. 6

p. 42   1.   6.

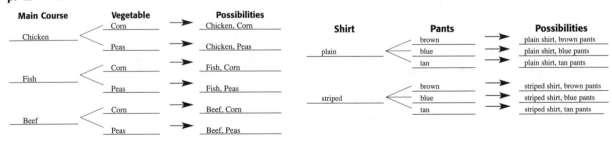

        2. 6, 3. 9, 4. 8

p. 44   1. Tom, 4 more, 2. 7 more

p. 45   (GP) 1. Carol, 5 more, 2. 2 more

Answer Key (cont.)

p. 46   (IP)

	Jenn	Jim	Kelly
red	5	6	6
yellow	4	2	1
green	6	8	10
blue	7	2	4

4, 2, 4 − 2 = 2, Jenn, 2, Jim; 1. Kelly. 2. 2, 3. 1, 4. 3

p. 48   1. 10 percent, 2. 20 percent, 3. November, February, April, 4. February–May

p. 49   (GP) 1. 1920, 2. 1840–1860, 3. 5 million, 1880, 4. Increase

p. 50   (IP) 1. 250 sales, 2. December, 3. August and September, 4. Check graphs., 5. October

p. 52   1. Felipe, 2. Mom, 3. 10, 4. 85

p. 53   (GP) 1. Wednesday, 2. Tuesday, 3. 20, 80, 60, 4. White Sea-Baltic, 5. 100 miles

p. 54   (IP) 1. 650,000 people, 2. 500,000 people, 3. Music Barn 45 CDs, 4. Jazz, 5. Melody Store 16 CDs, 6. 22 CDs

p. 56   1. Dragon; 2. Butterfly; 3. 1,377 feet; 4. Transamerica Pyramid; 5. 596 feet; 6. Empire State Building

p. 57   (GP) 1. Check tables, 2. Week 8, 3. Week 3, 4. Week 1, Week 7, Week 8, 5. Answers will vary.

p. 58   (IP) Totals: cheese-52, sausage-56, pepperoni-92; 1. 56, 2. Saturday, 3. Pepperoni, 4. $11.00, 5. 1 sausage and 1 pepperoni or 2 cheese and 1 pepperoni.

p. 60   1. 6, 0; 2. 1, 1; 3. 6, 0

p. 61   (GP) 1. 2, 1; 2. 6, 0; 3. 4, 6, 4; 4. 2, 0, 0; 5. 6, 12, 8; 6. 6, 12, 8; 7. 1, 0, 0; 8. 8, 18, 12

p. 62   (IP)

Figure	Faces	Edges	Vertices
Cube	6	12	8
Cone	1	0	0
Cylinder	2	0	0
Sphere	0	0	0
Rectangular Prism	6	12	8
Pyramid	5	8	5

p. 65-66 Answers will vary.

p. 68   Answers will vary.

p. 69   Answers will vary.

p. 72   From upper right, clockwise: condensation, evaporation, precipitation

p. 73   (GP) egg, caterpillar, chrysalis, pupa, butterfly emerging, butterfly

p. 74   (IP) Look at students' drawings.

p. 76   Answers will vary.

p. 78   (IP) 1. Accept reasonable classifications selections. 2. Answers will vary.

p. 81   (IP) Accept reasonable answers.

p. 84   1. United States map; 2. directions; 3. state capitals; 4. Ohio; 5. Mexico; 6. Florida

p. 85   (GP) 1. Pacific Ocean, 2. Golden Gate Bridge, 3. Yes, 4. Berkeley, 5. An airplane, 6. Palo Alto and Redwood City

p. 86   (IP) 1. Possible answers: Washington, California, Oregon, Idaho, Montana, Wyoming, Colorado, Utah, New Mexico, Arizona, South Dakota, Alaska, or Hawaii.; 2. Old evergreen forests; 3. Some parts have old evergreen forest, oak and pine forest, and some have little or no forests at all.; 4. Answers will vary.

p. 88   1. False; 2. True; 3. True; 4. True

p. 89   (GP) 1. Born near Reading, PA, 2. Moved to North Carolina, 3. Took part in the French and Indian War, 4. Married Rebecca Ryan

p. 90   (IP) 1. Letters left at inns, 2. Regular mail routes, 3. U.S. post office in *Constitution*, 4. Private carriers, 5. ZIP codes, 6. Fax and e-mail, 7.and 8. Answers will vary.

p. 92   1. chip; it's the guide word; 2. cactus, carrot; 3. no

p. 93   (GP) 1. Cross out boil, 2. Cross out kit, kung fu, 3. Cross out yourself, yak, 4. icicle, hydrogen, human, idea, howl, 5. journal, isn't, jacket, jeep, ivy, 6. kind, key, junk, kettle, just

p. 94   (IP) 1. 5, 2. 3, 3. 1, 4. Pronunciation, 5. 2

GLENCOE

The Basics of Speech

GLENCOE

The Basics of Speech

KATHLEEN M. GALVIN

Professor and Associate Dean

Communication Studies Department

School of Speech

Northwestern University

Evanston, Illinois

PAMELA J. COOPER

Professor

Communication Studies Department

School of Speech

Northwestern University

Evanston, Illinois

New York, New York   Columbus, Ohio   Chicago, Illinois   Peoria, Illinois   Woodland Hills, California

 Glencoe

The McGraw-Hill Companies

Printed in the United States of America

Send all inquiries to:
Glencoe/McGraw-Hill
8787 Orion Place
Columbus, OH 43240

ISBN: 0-07-866584-1

3 4 5 6 7 8 9 10 113 10 09 08 07 06

Contents

To the Student

No one can become a competent communicator simply by reading a book. Communicators need to think and consider, but they also need to *do* and evaluate the outcome. This means observing people and situations, analyzing information, and interacting with others.

As you complete the activities in this Workbook, you will do more than read and fill in the blanks. Each chapter will give you an opportunity to improve your skills.

As you apply the information from *The Basics of Speech*, you will learn more about how communication works. You will be well on your way to becoming a competent communicator. Enjoy the process!

Chapter 1
The Communication Process

1.1 Define It

The Key Terms in Chapter 1 explain the process and the types of communication. Read each of the following clues and determine the key word it identifies. Write the word on the blank at the right. Circle the part of the word or words that answers the italicized clue.

Key Terms

communication

group communication

interpersonal communication

interpretive communication

meaning

message

public communication

1. Within this word that means "the process of sending and receiving messages in order to share meanings," you'll find an *adult kitten*.

   _____

2. You *can't keep private* these words that mean "speaking before a large audience."

   _____

3. Within these words that mean "sharing meanings between people to build and maintain relationships," you will find the *singular of "people."*

   _____

4. The *opposite of down* is hard to find in these words that mean "participating together with a number of people for social or work purposes."

   _____

5. The *opposite of the prefix post-* is in this word that means "bringing literature to life for your audience."

   _____

6. There is a *muddle* or *confusion* within this word that means "how meaning is conveyed."

   _____

7. The *opposite of out* is in this word that means "the interpretation of a verbal or nonverbal message."

   _____

1.2 Communication Poster

Write the letters in the word *communication* down the left side of a piece of paper or on a piece of poster board. Then write phrases about the communication process or about your communication experiences for each letter. You can even try rhyme. For example,

C   ourage to say what makes you mad

O   bserving people who are happy and sad

M

M

U

N

I

C

A

T

I

O

N

1.3 Getting Acquainted

It is easier to discuss opinions and feelings with people you know. Get to know the other people in your classroom so that you will be more comfortable talking to them and in front of them. Ask your classmates to sign their names next to the categories that describe them. Each classmate may only sign your list up to three times.

CATEGORY   **NAME**

Volunteers time to community service   _____

Plays on a sports team   _____

Speaks a foreign language   _____

Plays a musical instrument   _____

Is taller than one parent   _____

Reads science fiction   _____

Collects Beanie Babies   _____

Has a part-time job   _____

Draws cartoons   _____

Can swim half a mile   _____

Sings in a performing group   _____

Has been to the White House   _____

Has been on television or radio   _____

Can do CPR   _____

Has run for school office   _____

Likes giving speeches   _____

Serves as a peer mediator   _____

1.4 Communication at Work

You may be surprised to discover the importance of communication in the workplace. Interview parents, neighbors, or friends about the way they communicate in their jobs. Find out the types of people they talk to, the kinds of messages they send and receive, and the way they use their skills. Write your conclusions using examples.

Person's Name   _____

Job Title   _____

People Communicated With   _____

                                     _____

Kinds of Messages   _____

                                     _____

Communication Skills   _____

                                     _____

                                     _____

                                     _____

Person's Name   _____

Job Title   _____

People Communicated With   _____

                                     _____

Kinds of Messages   _____

                                     _____

Communication Skills   _____

                                     _____

                                     _____

1.5 Meaning of the Message

Misunderstandings frequently occur because people do not have enough information. A good communicator tries to identify possible problem areas in a message and asks questions to get more or correct information. Read the following directions a parent might give a babysitter. Identify those parts of the messages that are unclear. Add four more unclear messages to the list and identify the problems. The first one is done for you.

DIRECTION

CONFUSION

1. Give the baby warm milk later.   <u>How much milk? How warm? When is later?</u>

2. Don't let Princess on the furniture.   _____

3. Watch Alice on the stairs.   _____

4. Call me if her cough gets worse.   _____

5. I'll leave my number on the table.   _____

6. We'll be home early.   _____

7. _____   _____

8. _____   _____

9. _____   _____

10. _____   _____

1.6 Interviews

Interview someone in your class. If you know the person well, try to find out six new things about this person that you did not know. If you do not know the person well, find out basic information, such as the person's interests, favorite books or movies, favorite music, part-time jobs, favorite sports, pet peeves, and hopes for a career. List this information below. Then use this information to introduce the person to the class.

Name _____

PERSONAL INFORMATION

1. _____

_____

2. _____

_____

3. _____

_____

4. _____

_____

5. _____

_____

6. _____

_____

Chapter ② Elements of Communication

2.1 Define It

The Key Terms in Chapter 2 refer to the essential elements in the communication process. Which one means "message expressed without words"? To find out, fill in the blanks with a word that fits each clue. After you finish, read the letters in the box to find the answer.

1. Interference that gets in the way of a message

2. Setting and people surrounding a message

3. Dictionary meaning of a word

4. Words used to communicate

5. How a message is transmitted

6. Explaining and interpreting sensations

7. Response to a message

8. An emotional response to a word

9. Informal language of a certain group

2.2 Motorist Symbols

Identify the following nonverbal symbols that are used on signs to alert motorists and pedestrians.

_____

_____

_____

_____

_____

_____

Now design some nonverbal symbols of your own. For example, you might want to warn your brother about entering your room or let your parents know that they have a phone call.

2.3 Reading Nonverbal Messages

Nonverbal messages are those expressed without words. They include appearance, facial expression, eye contact, posture, gestures, voice, and time/space/place. Describe the mood of the people in the photographs. Identify the nonverbal clues you used to make your decisions.

Picture 1

Mood: _____

_____

Nonverbal clues: _____

_____

_____

_____

_____

Picture 2

Mood: _____

_____

Nonverbal clues: _____

_____

_____

_____

_____

2.4 Perceptions

Because every person views the world slightly differently, no two people perceive the same message in the same way. To find out why, ask three people to respond to the following questions. Record the first person's answers on the lines. Use separate sheets of paper for the two other people.

1. What time is early in the morning? _____

2. Which food is not for dessert: *tamales,* _____
   baklava, stollen, kakor?

3. What is a great lunch? _____

4. What animal is small with a long nose _____
   and a tail that is naked and prehensile?
   It is mainly nocturnal and about the
   size of a cat. It is gray in color, and has
   coarse hair. If frightened, it may act
   dead.

5. What conclusions would you draw if _____
   you saw a classmate holding a map of
   South Dakota?

6. What would you mean if you told a _____
   friend that you needed more respect?

7. What do you see? _____

8. What would you do if you saw a road _____
   sign that said "Frost Heaves"?

9. What does a "tourist" look like? _____

10. What is an "adequate" income? _____

2.5 Word Exchange

The list at the left shows words that describe items, expressions, happenings, or activities that became well known in the 1970s. To show how new words or expressions enter the language, make a similar list of items, expressions, happenings, or activities that became popular in the 1990s.

1970s　　　　　　　　　　　　　　　　　1990s

1. skateboarding　　_____

2. windsurfing　　_____

3. corn rows　　_____

4. pet rocks　　_____

5. pocket calculators　　_____

6. the Muppets　　_____

7. Watergate　　_____

8. *Soyuz* 11　　_____

9. Legionnaires' disease　　_____

10. expressions like "far out"
    and "do your own thing"　　_____

2.6 Create a Context

Design the dining room of a restaurant in two ways. First, create a room that would discourage long conversations and very personal discussions. Then create a room that would encourage these kinds of conversations. Pay careful attention to distances between people and furniture type and placement.

Room 1: Impersonal

Room 2: Personal

2.7 Creating a Communication Model

Draw your own communication model using objects that represent sender and receiver and possible "noise" in the channel. For example, two paper cups connected by a string could represent sender and receiver. A pair of scissors might represent "noise" in the channel.

Sender

Receiver

"Noise" in the channel

Chapter 3
The Work of Speaking and Listening

3.1 Define It

The Key Terms in Chapter 3 refer to the processes of creating and listening to speech. Read each definition. Find and circle the word in the puzzle that fits the definition. You will find words vertically, horizontally, and diagonally.

1. the tube that carries air

2. hollow chambers that increase sound

3. act of receiving sound

4. voice box

5. characteristics of the speaker that interfere with listening

6. muscular sac between the mouth and the esophagus

7. environmental situations that keep you from paying attention to speaker

8. muscle separating the chest from the abdominal cavity

9. tongue, teeth, jaw, hard and soft palate, and lips

10. two elastic folds with a slit between them

11. process of receiving, interpreting, evaluating, and responding to messages

12. highness or lowness of speaker's voice

```
E X T E R N A L B A R R I E R S
O T A X E E A I H V O N R O R P
W E E T H D E L O H Q U S E P E
E V O C A L C O R D S B I C R A
P R A N D O E F M Y Z R L P S K
A R T I C U L A T O R S E G N E
T E R S E C I M M B N D N O T R
O S L A R Y N X B R N I G P M B
L O S T L A O T W I N D O N X A
A N A P P L L E T E G E T N A R
L A N I S E N D T E N D Y E T R
I T I T U O U S U A L R B R A I
H O N C Y S I T H E A R I N G E
T R E H S L I K E H E A T H B R
S S H E I D I A P H R A G M S S
```

3.2 Protecting Your Voice

Your vocal mechanism is delicate and must be cared for properly. Interview someone who needs to take special care of his or her voice—a singer, actor, auctioneer, radio announcer, or cheerleading coach, for example. What techniques does that person use to protect his or her voice? List the techniques.

Name _____

Occupation _____

Techniques _____

_____

_____

_____

_____

_____

_____

_____

_____

_____

_____

_____

_____

_____

3.3 Saying It Right

News announcers must learn to pronounce difficult words correctly. They practice saying names, places, titles, and other words that may not sound the way they are spelled. Read the following sentences and circle the words you find difficult. Look up their pronunciations and write out clues to help you remember these words.

1. The Hmong leader led the refugees from Thailand to a new community. _____

2. Seamus O'Connor and Sean O'Reilly will represent Ireland at the music festival in Paramus, New Jersey. _____

3. Giuseppe's luncheon menu includes minestrone, tortellini salad, eggplant parmigiana, and lasagna. _____

4. Fifteen ginkgo trees were planted in an arboretum in Baton Rouge. _____

5. This year there were speakers from Beijing, Shanghai, and Seoul. _____

6. Four persons were indicted Monday as ringleaders in the Thames River Valley extortion case. _____

7. Composers on this evening's program include Tchaikovsky, Shostakovich, and Rimsky-Korsakov. _____

8. The round-the-world trip included a stop in Pago Pago. _____

9. It seems likely that the ambassador committed a faux pas. _____

10. The recipe calls for Tabasco and Worcestershire sauces. _____

3.4 Listening to Spoken English

Spoken English may confuse listeners because some words are pronounced the same but have very different meanings. Therefore, a listener has to hear the word in context to understand the speaker's meaning. Words that are spelled and pronounced alike but are different in meaning and origin are called homonyms. For example, *bear* can mean "to support the weight of" and "any of a family of large, hairy mammals."

Give at least two short definitions for each word below. (You may use a dictionary.) Then write a sentence for each meaning of one of the homonyms. The sentences should contain enough context to convey the meanings accurately.

Definitions

1. fair _____

_____

2. pool _____

_____

3. maroon _____

_____

4. express _____

_____

5. post _____

_____

6. down _____

_____

Sentences

7. _____

_____

8. _____

_____

3.5 Recognizing Regionalisms

You have probably heard a word or expression used to refer to something that you know by a different name. For example, a *danish* in New York City might be called a *sweet roll* or *pastry* in Chicago. For each word or expression in column I, write the word or expression you use for the same thing in column II. (It may be the same word.) If you know of another word for the same thing, write it in column III.

I. Word or expression	II. Your word or expression	III. Other word(s), if any, for the same thing
1. soft drink	_____	_____
2. traffic circle	_____	_____
3. earthworm	_____	_____
4. creek	_____	_____
5. veranda	_____	_____
6. harmonica	_____	_____

3.6 Barriers to Listening

Keep a listening log for an entire day. Focus on the situations in which you didn't listen carefully, and record them below. Identify the barrier that broke your concentration. What occurred because of your failure to listen carefully?

Situation	Barrier	Effect
Example Mother told me to take my house key.	I was thinking about meeting Jenny.	I got locked out of the house.

3.7 Types of Listening in Context

Read the following statements. Identify the type of listening that you would
use in each situation. Would you listen for information, listen empathically,
listen critically, or listen creatively? Then describe a possible situation in
which each numbered item might be heard.

1. "Because of the lower tax base and increased school needs, our community is in trouble. We
   are long on people and short on cash. There are more children in your classrooms, but the
   businesses that provide tax money are moving away. Vote for Michael Gaven for Mayor. He
   will bring business back to Tinley City. He will make sure our children are well-educated."

Type of Listening _____

Possible Situation _____

2. "I really like Amara's idea for staging a play at the end of our unit on pioneers. We could show
   the pioneers of different times—pioneers at the time of westward expansion, women's rights, or
   space exploration. What other kinds of pioneers could we include?"

Type of Listening _____

Possible Situation _____

3. "I wish Pat would just leave me alone. He is always on my back about something. Everyone
   has a batting slump, but he doesn't understand. As junior coach, he thinks it is his job to push
   me until I get so angry that I clobber the ball. I don't need that kind of encouragement."

Type of Listening _____

Possible Situation _____

4. "Sharon Lubitz will tell us about her month-long trip to the Netherlands as a student
   ambassador. Sharon lived with a family in Amsterdam for two weeks, and then she traveled
   with the other student ambassadors throughout the countryside. She learned many Dutch
   customs and visited with many Dutch students. I am pleased to present Sharon Lubitz."

Type of Listening _____

Possible Situation _____

5. "Most of our campers like to fish, but not all the fish they catch are safe to eat. Campers must
   be careful of fish from waters that get runoff from garbage dumps or sewage treatment plants.
   The Ironside factory is located on the same lake as our camp. Therefore, I think we should be
   careful eating fish from the lake."

Type of Listening _____

Possible Situation _____

3.8 Put It in Writing

Many people with impaired hearing are excellent communicators, while many people who hear well are poor communicators. Why do you think this is true? The following poem may give you some ideas.

A Hearing Person in a Deaf World

Often and long have I wondered
How your silent world feels,
I've read and I've studied and learned a few things
But still, something is concealed.
My friend, standing there, I have watched you,
Trying to understand
The anger, the fear, the excitement
So clear on your face and your hands.
I who have learned so well to express
The same feeling and thoughts with my voice,
Must now teach these awkward hands to sign—
To join you, that's my choice.
Now I know I can never really enter
Your world, for in mind I am bound
But I understand, too, that the deaf world
Is as full with silence as mine is with sound.
                              —Elizabeth I. Wolter

What strengths and capabilities might help individuals with impaired hearing communicate?

_____

_____

_____

_____

What important communication lessons might hearing people learn from people with impaired hearing?

_____

_____

_____

_____

Chapter 4
The Competent Communicator

4.1 Define It

The Key Terms in Chapter 4 identify important ideas in the process of becoming a competent communicator. Read the following riddles. Write a Key Term after each one.

Key Terms

communication strategies   visualize   social rituals
competency steps   competent communicator   communication acts

Who Am I?

1. I am the informal rules or patterns for interaction.   _____

2. I am the verbal and nonverbal ways to share information, discuss feelings, manage persuasion, follow social rituals, and use imagination.   _____

3. I am the major reasons for communicating.   _____

4. I describe the process of imagining every move in one's mind before actually performing an act.   _____

5. I am a person who has developed strategies for dealing with communication situations and who follows the competency steps to be more effective.   _____

6. I describe the course of action that people with strong communication skills follow. The course of action includes thinking of strategies, choosing one, acting on it, and evaluating its effect.   _____

4.2 The Power of Persuasion

In order to persuade someone, you have to be clear about your own reasons for something and anticipate the other person's possible objections. Imagine that you have been assigned to do a book report. Your goal is to convince your classmates to read the book you have chosen.

(1) Choose a book, and then (2) list the reasons you chose it. What objections might your classmates have to reading your book? (3) List those objections next. (4) Finally, develop a strategy to persuade your classmates to read your choice. For example, you might want to report on J. R. R. Tolkien's *The Hobbit* because you like fantasy stories. Your classmates might object because they have heard that the names of the characters are difficult to remember. You might work out a list that would help others keep track of the characters. Or you might want to report on Gary Paulsen's *The Crossing* because you like realistic fiction.

Title of Book _____

Reasons for Choosing It _____

_____

_____

_____

_____

_____

Possible Classmate Objections _____

_____

_____

_____

_____

Strategy _____

_____

4.3 Learning Social Rituals

Much of everyday communication involves social rituals. How do people learn social rituals? Find out by watching parents and children communicate, perhaps in shopping malls, restaurants, or grocery stores. Record comments made by parents that relate to appropriate communication for social rituals.

People involved	Comments that relate to social rituals
Example: Mother to girl	"Please don't interrupt me when I am talking to someone."

4.4 Visualizing the Future

Competent communicators often rehearse in their minds what they will say or do in a particular situation. If you imagine yourself doing something correctly, you can help yourself prepare for the real situation.

Select a problem situation related to communication that you would like to handle better. Describe the problem in the Situation space. Write out the actions you hope to take and the statements you hope to make in the Visualization space.

People involved	Comments that relate to social rituals
Example: I am a Korean girl adopted into a Caucasian family. Sometimes strangers ask questions I don't want to answer. The next time someone asks, "Why did they adopt you?" or "What happened to your Korean family?" I will…	1. Look the person in the eye. 2. Say "Adoption is a family matter. We only discuss it in the family." 3. Change the subject by asking the person a question.

4.5 Increasing Your Range

In order to communicate more effectively in different situations, you should go through the following steps:

1. Determine your communication goals.

2. Consider the range of communication behaviors you can choose from.

3. Choose one behavior on the basis of the situation you are in. What seems right in this situation?

4. Act on your choice and perform the behavior.

5. Evaluate the success or failure of your message in terms of the receiver's response.

Select a situation that you have experienced already, or are going to experience, in which communication plays a big part. Go through the steps to reach a successful conclusion.

Communication Goal (What do you want to happen?) _____

_____

_____

Range of Communication Behaviors (What can you do? Brainstorm your options.)_____

_____

_____

Choice of Behavior (What are you going to do?) _____

_____

_____

Acting on the Choice (What did you actually do?)_____

_____

_____

Evaluation (How satisfied are you with the results?) _____

_____

_____

4.6 Adapting Your Language

Identify a situation in which you might give information to someone because you are knowledgeable on a subject. Write one paragraph using the language you would choose if that person has some experience on the subject. Write a second paragraph using language you would choose if the person does not know much about the subject. For example, how would you explain the process of making bread to someone who has experience in the kitchen and to a younger brother or sister?

Below are some suggestions to get you started.

How to prepare something   How to identify something
How to repair something   How to arrange something
How to build something   How to practice something

Situation_____

_____

_____

_____

Expert to Experienced Person _____

_____

_____

_____

_____

_____

_____

Expert to Beginner_____

_____

_____

_____

_____

_____

_____

4.7 Making Your Point

Prepare a two-minute speech for the class in which you have three or four main points. List your topic and main points below. Ask your classmates to take notes on the main points. When the speech is over, try to match your main points with the main points the listeners recorded. If there are any differences, try to find out what caused the confusion.

Example

Topic	How to Protect Your Belongings
Main Points	1. Don't carry much money.
	2. Don't leave wallet in your backpack.
	3. Don't leave your locker unlocked.
	4. Don't use cheap bicycle locks and chains.

Topic _____

Main Points 1. _____

_____

_____

2. _____

_____

_____

3. _____

_____

_____

_____

4. _____

_____

_____

_____

Chapter 5
Communication and Yourself

5.1 Define It

The Key Terms in Chapter 5 help you to understand the connection between your perception of yourself and your communication skills. To review this process, read each sentence, and fill in the blanks with the correct Key Terms.

Key Terms

self-concept	intellectual side	social side
physical side	self-esteem	

1   The messages other people send me influence the development of my _____.

2.   As part of my _____ _____ of self, I like to learn about sea mammals, especially dolphins.

3.   As part of my _____ _____ of self, I have two main sets of friends. I have friends from my church and friends from my neighborhood.

4.   As part of my _____ _____ of self, I pay attention to my weight by eating nutritious food.

5.   When my _____ is high, I tend to be more direct and honest in my communication with others.

5.2 A Strong Belief

Each year, groups of teenagers from the United States act as hosts to other teenagers from several war-torn countries. These groups tour parts of the United States to talk to other teens about injustice and war around the globe. If you had the opportunity to join a group expressing a strong belief, what group would you join? How would you express your beliefs to an audience?

Topic

_____

_____

_____

Group

_____

_____

_____

How I would express my beliefs

_____

_____

_____

_____

_____

_____

_____

5.3 Know Yourself

There are four basic steps to improving self-esteem. The steps are listed below. Try to follow the four steps in the process. First, evaluate yourself honestly. Then set realistic goals. Praise yourself, and finally, praise others.

1. Evaluate yourself honestly. Some examples are shown.

Strengths	Weaknesses
I listen to my friends.	Given a choice, I don't say what I'd like to do.

2. Set realistic goals.

I will try to say what I'd like to do 50% of the time.

3. Praise yourself.

4. Praise others.

5.4 How Others See You

Sometimes it's surprising to discover what other people think about you. A good communicator needs this information. If you asked your best friend, a parent, and a teacher to describe you, what do you think each person would say? You might expect your best friend to say that you are athletic and funny. You might think your mother would describe you as helpful but sloppy. You might expect your teacher to say you are outgoing but forgetful.

Choose three or four adjectives you think each person might use to describe you. Then ask your friend, parent, and teacher which words they would choose. Are there any differences between how you think others see you and how they actually see you?

How I Think Others See Me		
Best Friend	**Parent**	**Teacher**
How Others Actually See Me		
Best Friend	**Parent**	**Teacher**

5.5 Personal Renewals

Read the following introduction to an article on one young man's personal change that resulted in increased self-esteem and a willingness to reach out to others.

Students rebuild homes, their lives

By Laurie Goering

A year ago, Hyseal Shepherd's life was crumbling like the boarded-up mansions he walked past on his way to school.

Teachers described the 13-year-old as "one of the worst kids in school," a troublemaker at Price Elementary School with a bad attitude and less of an aptitude for spelling and math than for the toughs that ran his decaying Oakland neighborhood on the Near South Side.

It was an attitude shared by many of his classmates, who felt they had nothing to look forward to but poverty and joblessness in a dead-end neighborhood.

Not any more.

This year, Shepherd, a quiet and handsome 14-year-old in a Penn State sweatshirt, is at the top of his class in math and spelling and hasn't missed a day of school. He's quick to offer help to other students and was even named Citizen of the Month at Price earlier this school year.

"I feel like I'm somebody," he said, smiling. "I like coming to school now."

That's because this year, he and 34 other students have become pioneers in an unusual school program designed to turn around the poorest communities on the South Side by revitalizing both their people and their crumbling historic buildings. . . .

Using a newspaper or magazine article or personal observation, describe the before-and-after communication characteristics of someone else who made a significant positive life change.

Situation: _____

Previous Communication Patterns

_____

_____

_____

Current Communication Patterns

_____

_____

_____

5.6 Self-Logo

Clothes are frequently used as ways to let the world know something about you. Decorate this T-shirt to reflect the real you. Before you start, think about colors, slogans, and symbols. When you are finished, show your design and explain it to the class.

Chapter 6
Communication with Others

6.1 Define It

The Key Terms in Chapter 6 refer to the important parts of building friendships. Use them to label the following rhymes.

Key Terms

empathy   stereotyping   constructive criticism
first meetings   interpersonal communication

1. To put one's self in another's place
   Is to understand what that person will face.   _____

2. Any relationship's beginning stages
   May quickly fill your diary's pages.   _____

3. Feedback that helps a speaker improve
   Tells him or her how to keep in the groove.   _____

4. It's really not fair, that is my hunch,
   To label someone as "one of the bunch."   _____

5. If communication is very strong,
   A friendship can last a whole life long.   _____

6.2 Changing Friendships

When a relationship changes, moving either forward or backward, the verbal and nonverbal messages also change. A competent communicator pays attention to the changes. Analyze a friendship in which the individuals grew apart. Describe three or four changes in communication.

> **Example**
> Raoul and José always used to sit together at lunchtime. Now they sit at different tables in the cafeteria with new sets of friends. Sometimes you can see them look across at each other.

Situation: _____

Changes in Communication

1. _____

_____

2. _____

_____

3. _____

_____

4. _____

_____

5. _____

_____

6.3 Friendship in Action

If you examine your own friendships and those of people around you, the
six characteristics of friendship should stand out.

Characteristics of Friendship

1. Keeping secrets
2. Loyalty
3. Warmth

4. Support
5. Humor
6. Honesty

Select three of these characteristics. For each, describe an example of
communication behavior you have experienced or observed that shows
friendship. For example, you might be able to tell that two people are loyal
to one another if they don't talk behind one another's back.

1. Characteristic _____

   Example   _____

   _____

   _____

   _____

   _____

   _____

2. Characteristic _____

   Example   _____

   _____

   _____

   _____

   _____

   _____

3. Characteristic _____

   Example   _____

   _____

   _____

   _____

   _____

6.4 Communication Checklist

Use the following checklist to identify ways you talk with your friends. After completing the checklist, evaluate your responses. Think about ways you can be a better friend by improving communication.

	Always	Frequently	Sometimes	Never
1. I am comfortable talking to other people about personal things.	_____	_____	_____	_____
2. I often ask others how they feel about what I'm saying.	_____	_____	_____	_____
3. I am able to put myself in the other person's place, and I imagine what he or she is feeling.	_____	_____	_____	_____
4. I often check whether others really understand what I'm saying.	_____	_____	_____	_____
5. I can be trusted with other people's secrets.	_____	_____	_____	_____
6. When I feel hurt, I tell others how I feel.	_____	_____	_____	_____
7. I am usually able to say what I mean.	_____	_____	_____	_____
8. Other people come to me with their problems.	_____	_____	_____	_____
9. I try to be honest with my friends.	_____	_____	_____	_____
10. I stick up for my friends when others make fun of them.	_____	_____	_____	_____
11. If friends criticize my actions, I think seriously about their comments.	_____	_____	_____	_____
12. I am sure to find time to spend with my friends.	_____	_____	_____	_____

Ways I can be a better friend

_____

_____

_____

_____

_____

6.5 Removing the Mask

Many people wear "masks" to hide parts of themselves from others. As they develop friendships, they gradually drop these masks and share personal information. Describe the differences in behavior and communication between when a person wears a mask and when the mask is dropped. You may describe yourself, a friend, or a character in a book, movie, or television show.

"Masked" Behavior and Communication	"Unmasked" Behavior and Communication
Example: Shy; does not seem to have point of view about anything; always sits near the back of the room	Outgoing; expresses opinions with friends; usually sits near the front of the room

6.6 Putting On Another's Shoes

Empathy is the ability to put oneself in another person's place and understand what that person is feeling. Describe a situation in which you were able to do that and realize that person's feelings.

Example

Last summer our community center sponsored a summer production of *The Sound of Music.* The director brought a friend to auditions who kept making comments about the kids who were trying out. After one boy auditioned, this person announced loudly, "He can't play Friedrich. He's too fat, and he can hardly sing." That remark had to hurt. I would imagine the boy trying out felt very embarrassed and wished he could disappear into thin air.

Situation

_____

_____

_____

_____

_____

6.7 The Workings of Friendship

Using a friendship from real life, fiction, a movie, or television, describe incidents that indicate how this friendship is working. Describe the circumstances briefly below, and then explain the situation and your analysis to the class.

Example

Circumstances: Latanya and April were friends for six months. April became very sick with diabetes.

Analysis: This relationship remained strong because
1. Latanya was always careful to help April watch her diet.
2. Latanya never ate "problem foods" in front of April.
3. Latanya listened while April talked about her frustration.
4. Latanya searched the Internet to learn about diabetes.

Circumstances

_____

_____

_____

Analysis

_____

_____

_____

_____

_____

_____

_____

_____

Chapter 7
Communication in Groups

7.1 Define It
The Key Terms in Chapter 7 identify important parts of the group discussion process. Read each definition. Then complete the puzzle by filling in the letters of the Key Terms.

ACROSS

4. The final stage of the group life cycle
5. Standards for action within a group
8. Listing aloud as many ideas as possible before feedback occurs
11. A small number of people who share common interests
13. Person who keeps group process working and who makes sure everyone is involved.

DOWN

1. A method group members use to solve problems (two words)
2. Standards that a solution must meet to be acceptable
3. The first stage of a group life cycle
5. Stage when members start to function effectively together
6. Smaller unit within a group
7. The stage when groups confront differences
9. Subgroup whose members tend to stick together
10. A group's reason for existing
12. Personal pattern of communication characterizing one's place in group.

7.2 And This Could Be Used For . . .

Assume that you are alone and on foot in one of the following places: 1. a desert in southern Arizona in summer; 2. a snowy forest in Alaska in winter; 3. a deserted island without a boat off the coast of Maine. How many of the following items could you use to help you survive? In small groups, brainstorm to discover how creative you can be.

1. paper clip _____

_____

2. 2 rubber bands _____

_____

3. nail file _____

_____

4. newspaper _____

_____

5. wooden matches _____

_____

6. stick of gum _____

_____

7. piece of string _____

_____

8. mirror _____

_____

9. umbrella _____

_____

10. paperback book _____

_____

11. plastic rain hat _____

_____

12. felt tip pen _____

_____

7.3 Follow the Sequence

Effective problem solving involves following a sequence of steps. You need to identify the problem, analyze it, set criteria for solving the problem, develop solutions, and select a solution. The example shows how these steps work together to help group members solve a problem.

Think of a problem you have dealt with lately, or even a problem that you are working on now. Apply the problem-solving sequence to your problem in a group discussion. See whether you can come up with a workable solution to the problem. Use the worksheet on page 42.

Example	
Situation	You are part of a band that has been trying to get some good jobs. The group agreed to pay for the school sports banquet in order to get publicity. Five days before the sports night a local store owner asked the group to play at a grand opening of a second store because the original band canceled. The store is well known, and the owner will pay $150. The jobs are the same night.
Identify the Problem	How should the group handle the recent invitation?
Analyze It	The group wants publicity and money. The group committed to the sports banquet first. The banquet offers some publicity and no money. The store owner offers some publicity and money.
Set Criteria	The group wants publicity and money. The group wants a good reputation for business. The group wants more business.
Develop Solutions	The group plays the sports banquet. The group cancels the sports banquet to play at the store. The group tries to fit both into the same evening. The group splits up, and each subgroup adds a member so both events are covered.
Select a Solution	The group agrees to try to add two members so that both events are covered. If this does not work, the group agrees to keep the first commitment.

continued

7.3 Follow the Sequence (continued)

Situation

_____

_____

_____

Identify the Problem

_____

_____

_____

Analyze It

_____

_____

_____

Set Criteria

_____

_____

_____

Develop Solutions

_____

_____

_____

_____

_____

Select a Solution

_____

_____

_____

7.4 Something's Wrong

Below is an example of a group that is not working effectively. Also shown is an analysis of the member or leadership responsibility violated and what one group member would do to help solve the problems. Read the example, and then follow the same procedure to solve the problem below the example.

Example	
Problem	Our group isn't getting anywhere. Tomas keeps asking the same question over and over again. Everyone tries to talk at once, and Jessica, the moderator, doesn't say anything.
Analysis	Tomas is not a competent communicator because he violates the responsibility of asking questions appropriately. Jessica violates her leadership responsibility by not keeping the group on topic.
Solution	I would say, "Tomas, we answered that question already. Is something still unclear? Please, everyone, let's talk one at a time. Otherwise nobody can be heard." To help keep the group on the topic, I would say, "I don't see how what you are saying relates to what we are talking about. Could you explain how it relates?" If an appointed leader does not do the job, I guess I would try to.

Problem   Michael keeps interrupting and disagrees with everything Joel says. Joel, who has some really good ideas, has stopped talking in the group. Luisa, who seems shy, refuses to participate.

Analysis

_____

_____

_____

_____

Solution

_____

_____

_____

_____

7.5 The Nonparticipant in Group Discussion

What happens when one or more members of a small group don't participate? Sometimes such people almost seem like sticks of furniture just sitting there. With a partner, discuss what happens when people don't contribute. What happens to them? What happens to the group? How can nonparticipants be included? Write your conclusions below.

Effect on nonparticipants

_____

_____

_____

_____

Effect on group

_____

_____

_____

_____

Ways to get nonparticipants involved

_____

_____

_____

_____

_____

_____

7.6 Put It in Writing

Does your school have "in" groups and "out" groups? If so, what are some of the characteristics of each group? Write a paragraph describing these groups. Use the space below to brainstorm ideas for your paragraph.

_____

_____

_____

_____

Chapter 8
Forms of Group Discussion

8.1 Define It

The Key Terms in Chapter 8 identify elements in group discussion. Read each definition. Then complete the puzzle by filling in the letters of the Key Terms.

ACROSS

2. To refrain from voting
7. Situation in which subjects are explored by members in front of an audience (two words)
9. Written report of what happened at a meeting
10. Less than one-half of the voting members in a group
11. A proposed action for a group to consider
12. Group discussion during which members give short speeches to an audience

DOWN

1. Procedure for conducting group meetings, based on *Robert's Rules of Order Revised*
3. List of subjects to be discussed at a meeting
4. Within a larger group, a subgroup with a specific task
5. Format in which audience members participate in panel discussions and symposiums
6. To show support for a parliamentary motion
8. Name for a small group of audience members that discuss problems and reports solutions back to the larger group
10. More than one-half of the voting members in a group

8.2 Committee Observation

Observe a committee meeting in your school. Evaluate the committee using the following form. Using the following scale, rate each committee member.

Superior	Excellent	Good	Fair	Poor
5	4	3	2	1

Committee Members	Use of Material	Posture	Delivery	Cooperation	Preparation	Use of Reasoning	Participation	Enthusiasm (alertness)	Open-Mindedness	Knowledge of Subject

Overall rating for the group: _____

Comments

_____

_____

_____

_____

_____

_____

_____

8.3 What's Your Topic?

In groups of five to seven people, choose one of the following topics:

- Should the legal driving age be lowered nationally?
- Should public schools be allowed to require uniforms?
- Should students be required to perform community service?

Then participate with your group in a panel discussion on the topic you have chosen. Evaluate your participation using the following form.

Panel Topic _____

Rate the chairperson using this scale:

	Superior 5	Excellent 4	Good 3	Fair 2	Poor 1
Chair's Performance					
Introduction to the question					
Formal statement of the question					
Definition of terms					
Paraphrase of question					
Introduction of panel members					
Number of summaries					
Accuracy of summaries					
Distribution of time to panel					
Conclusions of panel discussion					

continued

8.3 What's Your Topic? (continued)

Rate the individual members, using this scale:

Superior	Excellent	Good	Fair	Poor
5	4	3	2	1

Panel Members' Performance	Use of Material	Posture	Delivery	Cooperation	Preparation	Use of Reasoning	Participation	Enthusiasm (alertness)	Open-Mindedness	Knowledge of Subject
No. 1 (Self)										
No. 2										
No. 3										
No. 4										
No. 5										
General Effectiveness:										
Overall Group Comments:										

8.4 Speak at a Symposium

In a group of four or five, prepare a twelve- to fifteen-minute symposium on a community or school issue. Select a topic that most people are generally familiar with. Break the topic into subtopics so that each person can speak for about two minutes.

For example, if your topic was "Improving Race Relations at our School," you might break the topic down into the following five areas:

1. What we need from our parents
2. What we need from our teachers
3. What we need from our community
4. What we need from our principal
5. What we need from each other

Each speaker in the symposium would address one of the areas.

Your Topic _____

Subtopics

1. _____

_____

2. _____

_____

3. _____

_____

4. _____

_____

5. _____

_____

8.5 Parliamentary, My Dear Watson

Parliamentary procedure helps meetings run smoothly. Understanding how the procedure works will help you communicate well in this small-group format. Read the following sample meeting. In the left margin, label the parts using the following terms: *adjournment, call to order, reading of minutes, old business, committee reports, reports of other officers, motion, discussion, amendment, second the motion, vote.* Some labels may be used more than once.

CHAIR: The meeting will come to order. Marcia will read the minutes of our last meeting.

MARCIA: The meeting of the Band Club was called to order by Melissa Martin on October 12, 1992, at 3:30 P.M. in Room 12 of Park School. The minutes of the last meeting were read and approved. Treasurer Jennifer Hoel reported that the club had $17.50 in the treasury. Under old business, the club discussed the advertising for the upcoming Band Day at school. Under new business, members discussed fund-raising projects. The meeting was adjourned at 4:30.

CHAIR: Thank you, Marcia. Are there any corrections or additions to the minutes? If not, the minutes are approved as read. Jennifer, please read the treasurer's report.

JENNIFER: We haven't spent or taken in any money since the last meeting. Our balance is still $17.50.

CHAIR: Thank you, Jennifer. Jaime, do you have a report from the Band Day Advertising Committee?

JAIME: Our committee is still trying to come up with a good slogan and a logo. We hope to have these ready for the membership to vote on at our next meeting.

CHAIR: Thank you, Jaime. On to old business. At our last meeting we talked about fund raising for the band trip. Anyone have any ideas? Shawonna?

SHAWONNA: I move we sell candy.

CHAIR: Calvin?

CALVIN: I second the motion.

CHAIR: It's been moved and seconded that we sell candy to raise funds for the band trip. Is there any discussion? Juan.

JUAN: Every club sells candy. People in my neighborhood are tired of buying candy. I don't think we'll sell any. Unless we can come up with something unique, I don't think selling candy will work.

BETSY: I agree with Juan. I know that at this time of year the only kind of candy that will sell is holiday candy. I move we amend the motion by changing *candy* to *holiday candy.*

continued

8.5 Parliamentary, My Dear Watson (continued)

CHAIR:	Margaret.
MARGARET:	I second the amendment.
CHAIR:	It's been moved and seconded to amend the motion by changing *candy* to *holiday candy*. Is there any discussion? Betsy.
BETSY:	Last year I was part of a group that sold candy wrapped especially for Hannukah or Christmas. We sold a lot for people to give as gifts.
CHAIR:	Jaime.
JAIME:	I really like that idea. But can we get the candy in time? It's already mid-October.
CHAIR:	Betsy, do you have any information on that?
BETSY:	It took our group three weeks to get the candy from the supplier. That would be just about the right time to start selling.
CHAIR:	Are there any more comments? (*Pause*) Since there are none, all those in favor of amending the motion by changing the word *candy* to *holiday candy* say yes. All opposed say no. The amendment is passed. Any discussion on the motion? Roberto.
ROBERTO:	I don't think we should sell candy at all. I think we should sell stationery or magazine subscriptions or something else.
CHAIR:	Responses? Kara.
KARA:	Roberto, I hope I don't offend you, but I have to disagree. The cheerleaders just sold magazine subscriptions to try and raise money for their new uniforms, and they didn't make much money. I don't know for certain, but I can't think who would buy stationery.
CHAIR:	Katie.
KATIE:	Call the previous question.
CHAIR:	Any objections? (*Pause*) If there are no objections, let's vote. It's been moved and seconded that we sell holiday candy to raise funds for the band trip. All in favor say yes. All opposed say no. The motion passes. Roberto.
ROBERTO:	It's almost 4:30. I move that we adjourn.
CHAIR:	Jennifer.
JENNIFER:	Seconded.
CHAIR:	It's been moved and seconded that we adjourn. All in favor say yes. All opposed say no. The meeting is adjourned.

Chapter 9
Introduction to Public Speaking

9.1 Define It

The Key Terms in Chapter 9 refer to public speaking and, in particular, to a special kind of informative speaking—the social ritual speech. Read each definition below. Then circle the letters in the puzzle that identify the Key Term for the definition. The letters can be vertical, horizontal, or diagonal.

1. Type of speaking in which one person addresses an audience for the purpose of informing or persuading

2. Speech in which the speaker's purpose is to increase the knowledge of the audience

3. Process of finding information about the audience that helps the speaker communicate with the members

4. Speech in which the speaker's purpose is to convince the audience to hold a certain belief or act in a certain way

5. Speaker's description of what a listener should be able to do after a speech is completed

6. Short informative speech that follows the same pattern every time it occurs

```
Q U E S T I O N A B L E C A L L S I N B
A S E B A L L B Y A N Y O T H E P R O N
E O S O C I A L R I T U A L S P E E C H
T H E R T H A N T H E U A M P I E R E T
H E W O R L D S E R I O E S A N C D T H
E W O R L D N E W S G S O T H A H T T H
S P E E C H T O P E R S U A D E T E P R
E S I D E N T H C A N D T H E C O N G R
E S A U D I E N C E A N A L Y S I S S C
A N A G R F E F O U R A Y A R E N I I T
N B C C B I S Q R T H M O P R T F Z U V
W Y N D D A D F G I J K P R U V O W Z T
L M P U B L I C S P E A K I N G R Y O U
L E A N T O W E S T E R N C I V M I L I
```

9.2 Speech Interest Inventory

Almost everyone has to give some kind of speech at some time during his or her lifetime. The following activities will help you prepare for giving a speech. When your time comes to speak, you will be ready. To help you decide on topics you would like to speak about, complete the following inventory. Read each item carefully. Write a speech topic for each item, and jot down any information you already know about it.

1. Experiences with animals _____

    _____

2. Hobbies and leisure-time activities _____

    _____

3. Events that affected my life _____

    _____

4. Vacations I liked (disliked) _____

    _____

5. Work I was paid for doing _____

    _____

6. The most interesting people I know _____

    _____

7. Books or films that I like (dislike) _____

    _____

8. What interests me the most about school _____

    _____

9. Places I've traveled (or would like to travel) to _____

    _____

continued

9.2 Speech Interest Inventory (continued)

10. Values I would fight for _____

    _____

11. Organizations or clubs to which I belong _____

    _____

12. Beliefs I hold about life _____

    _____

9.3 Analyzing an Audience

Learning to analyze your audience is important if you want to be a
competent public speaker. Choose a topic. Then analyze your audience—
your classmates—in relation to the topic you have chosen.

Your Topic _____

1. Basic Audience Data

_____

_____

_____

_____

2. Audience Beliefs and Opinions

_____

_____

_____

_____

3. Audience Knowledge of the Topic

_____

_____

_____

_____

4. Audience Expectations

_____

_____

_____

_____

Based on your answers to items 1 through 4, why do you think your
audience will be interested in your topic? _____

_____

_____

_____

9.4 Is an Audience Goal Like a Hockey Goal?

An audience goal describes what you want your audience to do after you speak. Practice writing audience goals by choosing one of the following topics:

- Explain the fun of skateboarding to a six-year-old who has never tried it, a teacher who thinks it is dangerous, or a friend who loves skiing.
- Explain your new high-tech stereo system to your science teacher, your friend who does not like music, or your younger sibling who wants to use it.
- Describe a movie you attended recently to your drama teacher, your parents, or a young sibling.

Now write an audience goal for each audience. Why is the goal appropriate for the audience?

1. Audience

_____

Goal

_____

Appropriateness

_____

2. Audience

_____

Goal

_____

Appropriateness

_____

_____

3. Audience

_____

Goal

_____

Appropriateness

_____

9.5 Speak About It

Identify the person you consider the most effective public speaker you have heard. Describe two reasons why this person is such a good public speaker. Give examples of what makes his or her speeches work so well. Then organize a short speech about the speaker.

The best public speaker I have heard is _____.

Reason 1 _____

Examples _____

_____

_____

_____

Reason 2 _____

Examples _____

_____

_____

_____

Chapter 10
Finding and Using Information

10.1 Define It

The Key Terms in Chapter 10 refer to the process of research and evaluation. Fill in the blanks in the dialogue with the correct Key Terms from the list.

Key Terms

cyberspace resources   opinion   supporting material
fact(s)   plagiarism   survey
interview   research

PAT: Hey, Ted. Why were you stopping people in class and writing down their comments in your notebook?

TED: I was doing _____. I'm taking a _____ of the cable TV shows that students in this school watch.

PAT: Sounds different. What are you doing after school?

TED: I'm going to _____ Andrea Gardner, Director of the Brier County Cable Network. I would like her _____ about the quality of cable shows here compared to those in other parts of the state. I also hope she can give me some _____ about the history of cable television in the state. I've also been searching the Internet.

PAT: Why are you doing all this work?

TED: Everyone in speech class has to give a final speech on a media-related topic. I chose cable television because I may want to work in that area some day. Right now I'm trying to put together my outline and _____. I collected some good quotes and statistics from students and some information from the Internet. I've got to make sure I'm not accused of _____ though.

PAT: Remember your old friends when you're a famous TV producer in Los Angeles. See you. I've got to find my own _____ for my paper on the rods and cones in a frog's eye.

TED: Cable sounds better all the time.

10.2 Report Support

Poor supporting material can ruin your speech. As you evaluate your
supporting material, you need to ask:

- Is it fact or opinion?
- Is it reliable?
- Is it relevant?
- Is it recent?

Imagine you are researching a speech about the rapid development of cities
in the Southwest. Which questions would you ask or comments would you
make about each of the following pieces of supporting material?

1. The Grand Canyon of Arizona is one of the most spectacular sights on earth. You can see it
    from the South Rim all year long. You can visit the North Rim in the summer months. The
    best way to visit the Canyon is by mule train or hiking.

    _____

    _____

2. Phoenix is the best city in the Southwest. It has great sports teams, lots of golf courses, and
    fine restaurants. I wouldn't live anywhere else.
        —Chris Tu, student, Arizona State University

    _____

    _____

3. "The threat of running out of water is most real in the western U.S.," Dr. Mohammed El-
    Ashry told *CONTACT*. He is a water resources expert. "If the population continues to
    increase, and if agriculture uses as much water as it does now, there will be problems."
        "Are We Running Out of Water?" Renee Skelton,
        3.2.1. *CONTACT*, July /August, 1987

    _____

    _____

4. The Native American population of Arizona has increased steadily since 1900, but its
    proportion relative to that of the state as a whole has decreased from more than 20 percent in
    1910 to less than 10 percent by the middle of the twentieth century.

    _____

    _____

10.3 What Do You Know?

A prepared interviewer is one who has done effective research. Imagine you have the opportunity to interview one of the following experts on his or her area of expertise. Circle the name of the person that you would like to interview. Then prepare four key questions you would plan to use during the interview.

Expert	Area of Expertise
Judy Blume	Writing for young people
Bruce Willis	Life as an actor
Michael Jordan	Life as a world-class athlete
Oprah Winfrey	Producing a TV talk show
Your school principal	Running a school
Ang Lee	Directing major films
Joan Ganz Cooney	Creating *Sesame Street*

Questions

1. _____

_____

2. _____

_____

3. _____

_____

4. _____

_____

10.4 Research Sources

As a researcher you need to be familiar with a wide variety of research sources. There is always one more place to look for information! What research sources might you use to find out the following information?

1. How to score tennis _____

   _____

2. The 1958 Chicago Cubs pitchers _____

   _____

3. The favorite lunch in your school cafeteria _____

   _____

4. The meaning and history of your full name _____

   _____

5. The childhood of Bill Cosby _____

   _____

6. The daily events on the day of your birth _____

   _____

7. The traffic outside school in the half-hour before the first bell _____

   _____

8. Academy Award winners in 1970 _____

   _____

9. The French word for *summer* _____

   _____

10. The author of *Maniac Magee* _____

   _____

10.5 Media Research

Imagine that you are going to give a speech that will include information gathered from a radio or television interview. Watch or listen to a documentary or interview show. Record two quotes or pieces of information that you think would be valuable to remember. Also mention any problems you had trying to gather information from radio or television

1. _____

_____

_____

_____

_____

_____

2. _____

_____

_____

_____

_____

_____

10.6 Finding and Using Supporting Material

Good supporting material helps a speaker develop a speech more fully.
Choose two of the following topics or two topics of your own. Give two
examples of supporting material you would look for when researching each
topic. Indicate one library research source and one computer research
source.

Earning Summer Money   How Children Learn Language
Drug Abuse and Health   Raising Pets
First Aid for Cuts and Bruises   Taking Good Photographs

Example

Topic: Expanding African Deserts

Library Research Source: map of deserts to show their expansion (visual aid); description of
changes in deserts since 1900.

Computer Site: http://members. aol.com/questsite/1/index.html

---

1. Topic _____

Supporting Material _____

_____

_____

_____

2. Topic _____

Supporting Material _____

_____

_____

_____

10.7 Fact or Opinion?

A good researcher must separate facts from opinions. Identify the following statements as fact or opinion. Rewrite five factual statements to make them opinions.

A.

    Fact Opinion

1. __ __ It is time for this nation to ban all indoor smoking.
2. __ __ Haven School has a tough attendance policy.
3. __ __ Country music is better than rock.
4. __ __ The price of cherries at the grocery store is $1.09 a pound.
5. __ __ If you have five unexcused absences at Central High School, you will flunk the class.
6. __ __ The Peace Corps was founded during John F. Kennedy's presidency.
7. __ __ Storytelling is becoming a popular art form.
8. __ __ Beans and squash are good sources of vitamins.
9. __ __ The Yellowjackets have won their first five games.
10. __ __ Neither film at the Gateway is worth seeing.

B.

1. _____

_____

2. _____

_____

3. _____

_____

4. _____

_____

5. _____

_____

Chapter 11
Constructing the Speech

11.1 Define It

The Key Terms in Chapter 11 identify important elements of speech construction. Label the following examples with the Key Terms that fit. You will use one Key Term twice.

Key Terms

simile	introduction	purpose statement
chronological order	personification	transition
metaphor	hyperbole	conclusion

1. Soccer is a valuable experience because it teaches athletic skills, keeps you in condition, and gets you involved in extracurricular activities. _____

2. Living in the Scottish countryside was like going through a time warp. _____

3. Who would want to spend hours in the blazing sun digging carefully in the dirt with a small spoon? I would! Last summer I spent two weeks at the Kampsville Dig. _____

4. The tree comforted the child in its branches. _____

5. On the other hand, the mayor has tried to solve the problem. _____

6. Please remember that seat belts save lives. They prevent serious injury. Wear seat belts. _____

7. Simmons hit the ball to the moon! _____

8. We are the urban pioneers. We circle our wagons around the city lot. _____

9. I'd like to tell you about a typical day on the Greek freighter *Constantine*, beginning at dawn. _____

10. The fog was a gray blanket shielding the sleeping gulls. _____

11.2 What's the Purpose?

Choose two of the following topics, or select two topics of your own, and write a purpose statement for each one. Make sure your purpose statement gives the topic of your speech, a guide to the way your speech is organized, and your audience goal.

Fads and Fashions   Prison Reform

Selecting a Career   School Disciplinary Policies

School Cliques   Analyzing a Film

Example

You should pay attention to fashion trends because fashion is both a way of expressing yourself and a reflection of the current concerns of society.

1. _____

_____

_____

_____

_____

2. _____

_____

_____

_____

_____

11.3 What's the Pattern?

Review the two topics and purpose statements you prepared for the "What's the Purpose?" activity on the previous page. For each of the topics, decide which pattern of organization—time, space, process, topical, problem-solution—works best. Explain your choices.

1. Topic _____

Organizational Pattern _____

Reason for Choosing _____

_____

_____

_____

_____

_____

_____

_____

2. Topic _____

Organizational Pattern _____

Reason for Choosing _____

_____

_____

_____

_____

_____

11.4 What's the Idea?

Choose one of your topics from the "What's the Pattern?" activity on the previous page. Using your purpose statement and organizational pattern, begin to organize the information for your speech. Refine your purpose statement if necessary, and identify the main ideas for your speech.

Example

Topic: Fashion

Purpose Statement: You should pay attention to fashion trends because fashion is both a way of expressing yourself and a reflection of the current concerns of society.

Main Ideas: I. Choosing Clothes
                   Mood
                   Attitude
                   Group Affiliation
              II. Reflection of Concerns
                   1950s—Bobby Socks; Long Poodle Skirts (self-satisfaction; fun)
                   1960s—Miniskirts; Stretch Pants; Bikinis (breaking rules)
                   1970s—Bell Bottoms; Layered Look; Platform Shoes (revolution; exploration)
                   1980s—Designer Fashions; Back to Miniskirts (money and self)
                   1990s—Split Skirts; Stirrup Pants; Biker Shorts (athleticism; do your own thing)

Your Topic:

_____

Your Purpose Statement:

_____

_____

_____

Your Main Ideas:

_____

_____

_____

_____

_____

_____

11.5 Creating an Outline

The next step is to arrange your speech into an outline. Using the organizational pattern and main ideas that you identified in the previous activities, outline your topic following the outline form below. You may create either a sentence, phrase, or word outline. (You do not need to write points or subpoints to fill all the spaces in the form.)

Topic: _____

Purpose Statement: _____

  I. _____

   A. _____

      1. _____

      2. _____

      3. _____

   B. _____

      1. _____

      2. _____

      3. _____

 II. _____

   A. _____

      1. _____

      2. _____

      3. _____

   B. _____

      1. _____

      2. _____

      3. _____

11.6 Put It in Writing

Introductions and conclusions are two important parts of your speech. Using your topic and purpose statement from the previous activities, write two introductions using two different methods: startling statement, rhetorical questions, humor, quotation, story, personal experience, example, or reference to the occasion, audience, or topic. Then write two conclusions using two different methods: summary, quotation, appeal, challenge, or story.

Read your introductions and conclusions to a small group of your classmates, and use their feedback to help you select the best ones.

Introduction 1

_____

_____

_____

_____

Introduction 2

_____

_____

_____

_____

Conclusion 1

_____

_____

_____

_____

Conclusion 2

_____

_____

_____

_____

Chapter 12
Delivering the Speech

12.1 Define It

The Key Terms in Chapter 12 are important terms in speech making. Which one identifies a method of delivery in which a speaker uses a prepared outline but does not plan each word and sentence? To find out, read each definition. Write the Key Term on the line at the right. Then circle the letter in the word that is indicated by the number in parentheses. Finally, arrange the letters in order in the blanks below to find the last Key Term. (You have been given two letters.)

Key Terms

manuscript	stage fright	memorized
media aids	clarity	pitch
volume	rate	impromptu
gestures	delivery	vocal quality

1. Nervousness when addressing an audience (5)   __ __ __ __ __   __ __ __ __ __ __

2. Clearness of a speaker's words (6)   __ __ __ __ __ __ __

3. Speed at which a speaker talks (4)   __ __ __ __

4. Delivery in which a speaker learns a speech and gives it word-for-word (1)   __ __ __ __ __ __ __ __ __

5. Highness or lowness of a speaker's voice (1)   __ __ __ __ __

6. Delivery in which a speaker talks without notes (5)   __ __ __ __ __ __ __ __ __

7. Way in which a speaker uses voice and body in giving a speech (7)   __ __ __ __ __ __ __ __

8. Sound or tone of a speaker's voice (4)   __ __ __ __ __   __ __ __ __ __ __ __

9. Nonverbal supporting materials, such as graphs and models (2)   __ __ __ __ __   __ __ __ __

10. Loudness or softness of a speaker's voice (2)   __ __ __ __ __ __

11. Movements of the head, shoulders, hands, or arms to emphasize a point (5)   __ __ __ __ __ __ __ __

12. Delivery in which a speaker writes out a speech and reads it (5)   __ __ __ __ __ __ __ __ __ __

The method of delivery is ___ X ___ __ __ __ __ __ __ ___ N __ __ __ __

12.2 Stage Fright Checklist

Stage fright affects different people in different ways. The trick to overcoming stage fright is to harness the energy and turn it to your advantage. The first step is to recognize how stage fright affects you. Complete the inventory below by checking the items that apply to you.

Bodily Reactions

___ rapid heartbeat	___ fast breathing	___ blushing
___ trembling hands	___ perspiring	___ feeling faint
___ eyes looking down	___ knocking knees	___ stomach butterflies
___ dry mouth	___ tense muscles	___ shaky voice

Nervous Habits

___ jingling coins	___ licking lips	___ rubbing or wringing hands
___ shifting feet	___ frowning	___ hands in pockets
___ clearing throat	___ pacing	___ playing with pens, jewelry, glasses

Mental Reactions

___ excessive worry	___ going blank	___ long, complicated sentences
___ mispronunciations	___ unrelated ideas	___ uhs, ers, ands, ums
___ slips of the tongue		

Now that you know how stage fright affects you, list three ways to help yourself build confidence. Try to address specific symptoms of stage fright.

Example I will leave my pencil at my desk so I won't play with it.

1. _____

_____

_____

2. _____

_____

_____

3. _____

_____

12.3 Special Delivery

This activity has several parts. Try to do all of them so that you can focus on the way you want to deliver your speeches.

A. Read the following sentences as indicated. *F* stands for *fast*; *S* stands for *slow*. Then read them again the opposite ways. Be sure to lengthen the sounds, not the pauses, when you go slow; work for clarity when you speed up.

- There are too many students in here already. (F)
- It's so quiet and peaceful out here in the backyard now. (S)
- I'm already late, and the car won't start. (F)
- No one is to leave without permission. (S)
- Late in the evening the rain came slowly, pelting softly on the fresh-turned earth. (S)

What is the effect on the meaning of some of the sentences when you reverse the instructions? For example, the fourth sentence sounds angry when it is read fast.

1. How does the meaning of the first sentence change when read slowly? _____

2. How does the meaning of the second sentence change when read fast? _____

3. How does the meaning of the third sentence change when read slowly? _____

4. How does the meaning of the fifth sentence change when read fast? _____

B. Read the following sentences, changing the volume as indicated. What logical meaning can you find for each reading?

Example

Statement	**Logical Meaning**
YOU can eat strawberries in June.	You can, but I wouldn't
1. You CAN eat strawberries in June.	_____
2. You can eat STRAWBERRIES in June.	_____
3. You can eat strawberries in JUNE.	_____

continued

12.3 Special Delivery (continued)

C. With a partner, practice saying the boldfaced words to communicate the meanings given below them. Use only your voice, not your facial expressions, to show meaning.

Uh-Huh

So that's what you've been up to! (angry)
I'm trying to be polite, but I want to concentrate on this book.
Yes, indeed! I love it!
You didn't think that I knew that, did you?

Maybe

There's a good chance we can go!
I don't really have any hope.
What do you mean *maybe*? I'm positive!
Don't bother me right now.

Sure

I don't believe you for a minute.
Definitely!
How can you doubt it?
I'm trying to think positively, but I'm doubtful.

Jane

Come here, please.
Is that you?
No, it can't be.
You'd better stop that right now!

What did you learn about your voice? Consider rate, volume, pitch, vocal quality, and clarity.

_____

_____

_____

_____

_____

_____

_____

Source: "Resource Materials for Speaking and Listening in the Secondary Language Arts Program," Corpus Christi Independent School District, Corpus Christi, TX, 1985, pp. 28–29.

12.4 Rehearsal Sessions

Understanding how you rehearse can help you improve your speech performance. There are many ways you can rehearse for the speeches you will present in class. Keep a log of your rehearsal schedule for one of your speeches.

Time/Date	Place	Minutes of Practice	What I Did
10/18 8 P.M.	My bedroom	15	I read over my speech several times.
10/19 7:15 P.M.	The kitchen	20	I delivered my introduction and first 2 points for my mother.

12.5 Visualizing Your Message

Sometimes a speech requires a visual aid to be effective. Describe or sketch a visual aid that could be used for the following speech topics.

1. Karate Moves

2. Tracing Your Family History

3. Using a Video Camera

4. Collecting Postage Stamps

5. Famous Public Speakers

Chapter 13
Creating the Informative Speech

13.1 Define It
The Key Terms in Chapter 13 identify parts of the speech-making process.
Read each clue below. Then write the Key Term that fits the clue.

Key Terms
critic   connected information   informative speech

critique   informal feedback   formal feedback

social-ritual speech   eulogy   constructive criticism

1. I am a two-word term that means "new information that is related to information the audience already knows." _____

2. I am a two-word term that means "a speech presenting factual or descriptive information." _____

3. You don't have to speak French to identify me. I mean "formal feedback given by a critic to a performer." _____

4. Both my words begin with the same consonant. I mean "feedback that tells a speaker what worked, what can be improved, and how to improve it." _____

5. I am the verbal and nonverbal feedback that is given spontaneously to a speaker. _____

6. What I do is judge or evaluate. _____

7. You don't have to wear a tuxedo to identify me. All you have to do is plan your comments (written or oral) that are intended to affect a speaker's next performance. _____

8. I am a three-word term that means "a short informative speech that follows the same pattern every time." _____

9. I am a speech given to honor a person who has died. _____

13.2 Design an Invention

Invent and design an object that would be useful or fun. For example, in
order to practice giving information clearly and concisely, design a new toy.
Consider the way it works, how much it will cost, and what age group it will
be for. After you have thought about your toy, draw it in the box below.
Then explain your new product to a partner.

How Invention Will Work

_____

_____

_____

_____

_____

Age Group or Audience for Invention

_____

_____

Cost of Invention

_____

Invention Design

13.3 Advertise Your Invention

Create an advertisement for the invention you designed on the previous page. Use the principles of informing; create a need to know, use connected information, organize the information well, and use repetition and memorable images. Don't overload your audience with too much information. Use a visual as well as a verbal message.

Visual Message

Verbal Message

_____

_____

_____

13.4 Let Me Tell You

Choose a topic and prepare an informative speech. Incorporate all the speech techniques you have learned in Chapters 9 through 12, including the rehearsal techniques. Answer the questions below as you begin to organize your speech. Then prepare an outline.

1. General Information

    A. Speech topic _____

    B. Audience Goal _____

    C. Purpose Statement _____

    D. Organizational Pattern _____

    E. Why This Pattern Is Appropriate _____

2. Audience Analysis

    A. Who is your audience? Give their educational background, age, sex, and so forth.

    _____

    _____

    B. Why will your audience be interested in your topic?

    _____

    _____

    C. What does your audience know about your topic?

    _____

    _____

    D. What is your audience's attitude toward your topic?

    _____

    _____

3. Content

    A. What supporting materials will you use? Why have you chosen them?

    _____

    _____

    B. What type of reasoning will you use? Why?

    _____

    _____

13.5 Creating the Social-Ritual Speech

A social-ritual speech is a special type of informative speech—one that follows a set formula or pattern. Listen to a social-ritual speech either at your school or in the community. Evaluate the speech using the following form.

Speaker _____

Social Ritual _____

1. Was the tone and style of the speech appropriate to the social ritual? Why?

_____

_____

_____

_____

2. Did the language and delivery of the speech fulfill audience expectations for the social ritual? How?

_____

_____

_____

_____

3. What was the major strength of the speech?

_____

_____

_____

_____

4. What was the major weakness of the speech? How could this be improved?

_____

_____

_____

_____

13.6 Put It in Writing

Imagine that your best friend just gave an informative speech about the way
to make a family tree. Your friend used the process order of organization,
talked much too fast, used good eye contact, and had some examples of
family trees that were too small for the audience to see clearly. Using the
principles of constructive criticism, write three points that you would tell
your friend, giving both comments and examples.

1. _____

_____

_____

_____

_____

_____

_____

2. _____

_____

_____

_____

_____

_____

_____

3. _____

_____

_____

_____

_____

_____

_____

Chapter 14
Creating the Persuasive Speech

14.1 Define It

The Key Terms in Chapter 14 refer to important parts of the persuasion process. Which one refers to using specific pieces of information to reach a general conclusion? To find out, read the definitions at the left. Then write the Key Terms. Circle the letters that are indicated by the numbers in parentheses. Finally, write the circled letters in order on the blanks below.

Key Terms

persuasion   bandwagon appeal   ethical decisions
name calling   deductive reasoning   faulty reasoning
inductive reasoning   testimonial   unrelated testimonials
persuasive speaking   card stacking   glittering generalities
impact   cause-effect reasoning

1. The major effect of a speech (1) _____

2. Suggestion that you should do something because everyone else is doing it (3) _____

3. Using a general idea to reach conclusions about specific instances (3) (4) _____

4. Decisions that have to do with right and wrong (5) _____

5. An opinion expressed by a well-known person on a particular subject (1) (5) _____

6. Talking to an audience to convince or persuade listeners (9) _____

7. Attacking a person rather than the person's ideas (4) _____

8. Changing a listener's beliefs or moving a listener to action (3) _____

9. Suggesting one event produces another (6) _____

10. Incorrect reasoning (2) (10) _____

11. Linking positive feelings for one thing or person to an unrelated thing or person (16) (17) _____

12. Piling up information in favor of ideas, without support (10) (11) _____

13. Vague statements (11) _____

___ ___ ___ ___ ___ ___ ___ ___   ___ ___ ___ ___ ___ ___ ___ ___ ___

14.2 Identifying Listener Needs

Competent persuaders try to learn how to relate to listener needs. As a listener, you should be able to analyze such persuasive appeals. Using Maslow's need pyramid, identify the needs to which the speaker is appealing in each of the following statements.

Maslow's Pyramid of Needs

Self-Actualization
Self-Esteem
Belonging
Safety
Physical

Higher-Level Needs

Most Basic Needs

Statement	Need
1. If we don't control air pollution, we can destroy the human race.	_____
2. Get a programming job, and you can get that house large enough for your family.	_____
3. Show up for Saturday's game and be a part of the Hillsboro Homecoming Holiday.	_____
4. Take a foster child into your home and enrich both your lives.	_____
5. Being on the honor roll puts you on the top.	_____
6. Buckle up and protect yourself from thoughtless drivers.	_____
7. Create your own holiday cards and share your talents.	_____
8. Don't be the last family on the block to own digital television.	_____

14.3 Making Yourself Believable

As a persuasive speaker, you must learn how to "sell yourself" to an audience. Select two topics and describe how you might make yourself believable while speaking persuasively about each one.

Topic 1

_____

Your knowledge, connection, or interest

_____

_____

_____

_____

_____

_____

_____

_____

Topic 2

_____

Your knowledge, connection, or interest

_____

_____

_____

_____

_____

_____

_____

_____

14.4 Understanding Listeners

One way to discover how people are persuaded is to study buying habits.
Interview three of your friends about recent purchases of items such as
makeup, sports equipment, clothes, or tapes. Try to find out the persuasive
messages that influenced their purchases.

Example

Person: female, 14 years old

Purchase: Nicole and Strom shirt

Reasons: Everyone is wearing Nicole and Strom shirts. I like the way they look. The quality is
good, and the price is right.

---

1. Person _____

   Item _____

   Reasons _____

   _____

   _____

   _____

2. Person _____

   Item _____

   Reasons _____

   _____

   _____

   _____

3. Person _____

   Item _____

   Reasons _____

   _____

   _____

   _____

14.5 It Sounds Reasonable

Identify the following statements as examples of inductive (I), deductive (D), or cause-effect (CE) reasoning. Remember that deductive reasoning reasons from the general to the specific; inductive reasoning reasons from the specific to the general.

	Example
_D_	The debaters are the smartest students in the school. I guess Dorene must be smart because she is a member of the debate team.

————— 1. Ten years ago, 700 houses in town had smoke alarms, and we had 35 serious injuries from fires. Last year, 4,500 homes had smoke alarms, and we had 12 serious injuries. The smoke alarms really prevent injuries from fire.

————— 2. If you feed your dog Bowser Bits, your dog will have strong canine bones.

————— 3. Two of the restaurants I go to are decorated in red or orange. These must be the colors that get people to eat a lot.

————— 4. Lakewood is a wealthy suburb. Since Courtney lives in Lakewood, her family must have plenty of money.

————— 5. Brushing with Glare will prevent cavities and gum disease and whiten your smile.

————— 6. Tim has practiced his song for two weeks. He will surely get the lead in the musical.

————— 7. Good speakers use many examples. Akeem must be a good speaker because he made his point well through examples.

————— 8. *Julius Caesar* is required reading in sophomore English. Andy has just completed his sophomore year; therefore, he must have read *Julius Caesar*.

————— 9. It has rained for my first five days in Seattle. I had better buy an umbrella.

————— 10. Lots of people have allergies in the spring. Peggy has been sneezing all week. She must be allergic.

14.6 Creating a Persuasive Outline

Imagine you have to give an impromptu persuasive speech. You have been given five minutes in class to create an outline. Select one of the following topics and write a purpose statement. Then outline your message using key words and a problem-solution organization.

Allowances	Being a Teen	Gym Class
Cafeteria Food	Smoking	Year-Round Schooling
School Dress	Drinking	Rock Concerts

Topic: _____

Purpose Statement: _____ is (are) a problem

because _____.

I believe we can solve this problem by _____

_____.

I. Problem _____

    A. _____

        1. _____

        2. _____

    B. _____

        1. _____

        2. _____

II. Solution _____

    A. _____

        1. _____

        2. _____

    B. _____

        1. _____

        2. _____

15.4 A Matter of Value

Lincoln-Douglas debate involves value propositions. To give you experience with this type of proposition, do the following exercise. Choose four subject areas from those below and write a value proposition for each. Remember that a proposition of value is a statement that says something is good or bad, right or wrong, useful or useless.

Music   Cheating on Exams
Rights of Criminals   Coeducational Sports Teams
Environmental Issues   Gun Control

1. _____

_____

_____

_____

2. _____

_____

_____

_____

3. _____

_____

_____

_____

4. _____

_____

_____

_____

15.5 Debate in Action

Pair up with a classmate to form a team and stage a mini-debate with
another team. Choose an issue to debate, and write a proposition. One team
will argue the affirmative side; the other will argue the negative side. Each
mini debate should include a two-minute constructive speech by each side,
a o minute affirmative rebuttal, a two-minute negative rebuttal, and a
on inute second affirmative rebuttal. Present your mini-debates for the
cl d ask your classmates to judge which side won the debate.

_____

n _____

_____

-Debate _____

_____

_____

_____

_____

_____

_____

_____

_____

_____

_____

_____

_____

Winning Side _____

Reason for Decision _____

_____

_____

Chapter 16
Preparing for Oral Interpretation

16.1 Define It

The Key Terms in Chapter 16 identify the main ideas to remember when preparing for oral interpretation. Which one means "the art of reading literature aloud to communicate meaning to an audience"? To find out, fill in the blanks with a word or term that fits each clue. After you finish, read the letters in the boxes to find the answer.

Key Terms

conflict	onomatopoeia	plot	setting
dramatic speaker	oral history	rhyme	style
mood	oral interpretation	rhythm	theme

1. Emotional feeling of a piece of literature
    __ [R] __ __

2. Voice that is heard telling the story or poem during a reading
    __ __ [L] __ __ __ __ __ __ __ __ __ __ __ __

3. Time and place of a piece of literature
    __ __ __ [N] __ __ __

4. Main idea of a piece of literature
    __ __ __ __ __

5. Way that a piece of literature is written
    __ __ __ [R] __

6. Story line
    [R] __ __ __

7. Words that sound alike
    __ __ __ __ __

8. Pattern of stressed and unstressed syllables
    __ __ __ __ __ __

9. Words that sound like their meaning
    __ __ __ __ [T] __ __ __ __ __ __

10. Struggle at the heart of most literature
    __ __ __ __ __ __ __ __

11. Stories told over and over again and passed down through the generations without being written down
    [N] __ __ __ __ __ __ __ __ __

16.2 Literature Log

The first step in preparing for oral interpretation is finding material that you like and that will work well for an audience. Begin keeping a log of literature that is suitable for oral interpretation. For each selection you find, record the following information: title, author's name, type of literature, source of piece, and comments about why the piece will work well for oral interpretation.

Example	
Title	The Fable of the Discontented Fish
Author	Fulani oral tradition (from Senegal)
Type of Literature	Folktale
Source	World Myths and Legends by Joanne Suter
Comments	A good story to read to young children

Use this as a model for your literature log form.

Title _____

Author _____

Type of Literature _____

Source _____

Comments _____

_____

_____

_____

16.3 Selecting Literature

Analyze the following poem in relation to the four standards of selecting literature—quality of the material, audience analysis, oral possibilities, and your feelings for the piece. Would this poem work well for oral interpretation? Why or why not?

Alone

Lying, thinking
Last night
How to find my soul a home
Where water is not thirsty And bread loaf
    is not stone…

I came up with one thing
And I don't believe I'm wrong
That nobody,
But nobody
Can make it out here alone.

Alone, all alone
Nobody, but nobody
Can make it out here alone.

There are some millionaires
With money they can't use…
Their wives run round like banshees…
Their children sing the blues.
They've got expensive doctors
To cure their hearts of stone.

But nobody,
No nobody
Can make it out here alone.

Alone, all alone
Nobody, but nobody
Can make it out here alone.

Now if you listen closely
I'll tell you what I know…

Storm clouds are gathering…
The wind is gonna blow…
The race of man is suffering
And I can hear the moan,

Cause nobody,
But nobody
Can make it out here alone.

All, all alone

Nobody, but nobody
Can make it out here alone.
        —Maya Angelou

Quality of Material _____

_____

Audience Analysis _____

_____

Oral Possibilities _____

_____

continued

16.3 Selecting Literature (continued)

Why would this poem work well for an interpreter?

_____

_____

_____

What difficulties would the poem present for an interpreter?

_____

_____

_____

16.4 Analyzing Literature

In order to be an effective oral interpreter, you must be very familiar with your literature. You must thoroughly analyze it. Choose a piece of literature from your literature log and analyze it using the form below.

Title _____

Author _____

Setting _____

Characters _____

Dramatic Speaker _____

Conflict _____

Climax or Turning Point _____

_____

Mood/Atmosphere _____

_____

Major Theme _____

_____

I like this selection because _____

_____

I think this selection is good literature because _____

_____

Describe the physical characteristics of the main character. _____

_____

Describe the emotional or mental characteristics of the main character. What kind of person is he or she?

_____

_____

What figures of speech and other elements of style are particularly good?

_____

_____

16.5 Oral History

A valuable source of material for oral interpretation is family stories. Stories are passed through the generations. One student learned the following story from her 80-year-old grandfather:

I remember the first automobile in our town. The whole town came out to see it. The people who owned the car charged a penny to ride in it. I remember how I begged my father to buy a car. It was a real status symbol. If your father owned an automobile, you were someone special!

Ask a relative to tell you some family stories. Write down your favorite. Also record something about the person who told it to you.

My Favorite Family Story

_____

_____

_____

_____

_____

_____

_____

_____

_____

_____

_____

The Storyteller

Name_____

Age _____ Relationship to Me _____

What I Like Best About This Person _____

_____

_____

16.6 Put It in Writing

Suppose you are on a speech team that travels around your community performing literature as entertainment. Below are descriptions of sample audiences. Describe the kind of literature your group should prepare to perform for them. Give reasons for your choices and provide examples.

Example	
Elementary School PTAs	This group would like to hear stories they could read or tell to their children. Use some recent literature they may not know, and then remind them of some old favorites. In our community, multicultural literature should be performed. Possible stories: "The Elephant's Child" or "The Nightingale."

The local nursing home　　　　　　　　_____

_____

The junior high school Young Authors meeting　　_____

_____

The kindergartners in a local school　　　　_____

_____

The Retired Teacher's Association　　　　　_____

_____

Hospital Children's Ward　　　　　　　　_____

_____

The Rotary or Kiwanis Business Luncheon　　_____

_____

Chapter 17
Performing Oral Interpretation

17.1 Define It

The Key Terms in Chapter 17 refer to performing oral interpretation. Read each couplet below. Then write the Key Term that best expresses the idea in the verse.

Key Terms

body recall   eye focus   sense recall
cutting the literature   marking the script   storytelling

1. Write symbols in the script to help you remember
   How to read the word *December*.   _____

2. This is the place that you can look
   While interpreting a poem or a part of a book.   _____

3. Use your theatre performance skills
   To create the feeling of winter chills.   _____

4. Take out the art you do not need
   To help the listener with the piece you read.   _____

5. You may create the sounds of a whale
   As you are involved in presenting your tale.   _____

6. If you can recall when you acted wary,
   You can interpret a scene that's scary.   _____

17.2 Creating an Introduction

Choose a poem that is suitable for oral interpretation. Using the guidelines for a good introduction, write an introduction for your poem on a separate sheet of paper. Your introduction should capture the attention of the audience; tell the author and the title; give necessary background information about the author or the piece of literature; set the scene; and tie the selection to the audience's experience, if possible.

17.3 Sense Recall

Sense recall is remembering experiences you have had that help you suggest images to your audience. Read each of the following phrases and describe them using your sense recall. Describe how they smell, taste, feel, look, or sound.

1. A sneeze

   _____

   _____

2. Chalk scraping on a chalkboard

   _____

   _____

3. A chain saw

   _____

   _____

4. The sound made by a frog

   _____

   _____

5. A fire in a fireplace

   _____

   _____

6. Ice cubes under a water faucet

   _____

   _____

7. Rollerblades on a sidewalk

   _____

   _____

8. A hot fudge sundae

   _____

   _____

9. A subway station

   _____

   _____

10. A fast-food restaurant

   _____

   _____

17.4 Using Your Body and Voice

Competent oral interpreters use their voices and bodies in interpreting literature. What movement, vocal variety, facial expression, and eye focus would you use to interpret the following selection?

The Boastful Bullfrog and the Bull

A Bullfrog lived in a little bog. He thought himself not only the biggest thing in the pond but the biggest thing in the world.

"I am not like other frogs," he told anyone who would listen. "I am the biggest thing of its kind. That's why they call me a Bullfrog. I am to other frogs what a Bull is to little calves."

He had heard about Bulls, but he had really never seen one. Then one day an enormous Bull came down to the pond for a drink. For a moment the Bullfrog was startled, but it did not take long before he was as conceited as ever.

"You think you're big, don't you?" he said to the Bull. "Well, I can make myself just as big as you."

The Bull said nothing. He barely looked at the croaking creature.

"You don't believe it?" said the Bullfrog. "Just you watch!"

He blew himself up to twice his size. The Bull still ignored him.

"Not big enough?" croaked the Bullfrog. "I can make myself still bigger. See!"

This time the Bull made a scornful sound and turned his head away.

This was too much for the Bullfrog. He took a huge breath and blew, and blew, and blew himself up—until he burst.

Moral: Don't try to seem bigger than you really are.

　　　　　　　　　　　　　　　—Adapted by Louis Untermeyer from *Aesop's Fables*

Movement _____

_____

_____

Vocal variety _____

_____

_____

Facial expression _____

_____

_____

Eye focus _____

_____

_____

17.5 Marking the Script

Read and analyze the following poem. Mark the script as you would if you were to read it aloud. Then read the poem to a classmate. Ask for a critique. How might you change the markings to improve your performance?

Moving Day

Crates
   full of my childhood
   stand by the door.
My mother's dishes are packed carefully;
   breaking them would mean losing part of our past.
The pale green curtains
   (the ones I picked out)
hang silently in the empty room.
Laughter—
   tears—
      talking—
the sounds of growing up
echo in the hallways.
Home.
New people will grow up here,
   will experience love and pain here;
this home will always be a home.
Our story will continue elsewhere;
We will still share laughter, tears, talking—
Love.
Boxes
   full of memories
   are being loaded into the car.
We will unpack these memories
   and use them to create
   a new Home.
   But a part of me stays behind,
   watching my pale green curtains
   swaying in a warm breeze.
            —Margaret Susan George

17.6 Personal Storytelling

Every person makes choices in life that involve moving in one direction while giving up the chance to go another way. You may have decided to go out for soccer, but you had to give up piano lessons. Your family may have decided to move to a bigger house, but you lost your friends from your old neighborhood. These important decisions or choices are sometimes called "forks in the road," and they may have stories attached to them. Select an example of a "fork in the road" situation from your own life, or one from the life of a real or historical person. Create a story out of this situation, and tell it to the class. Use this sheet to help you prepare.

The Decision

_____

_____

Background

_____

_____

_____

_____

_____

Pros and Cons of the Decision

_____

_____

_____

_____

_____

Results of the Decision

_____

_____

_____

17.7 Evaluating Storytelling

Listen to your classmates telling their stories, and select one storyteller to evaluate carefully. Write your comments for each category, and evaluate the speaker's overall performance.

Storyteller _____

1. *Choice of Selection:* Appropriate for audience? Why?

    _____

    _____

    _____

2. *Voice and Diction:* Voice quality, tone, pitch, rate, and range motivated by mood of the selection? Technique smooth? Pronunciation accurate? Volume appropriate?

    _____

    _____

    _____

3. *Use of Body:* Limited gestures or broad movements? Did speaker appear poised and self-confident? Did speaker avoid distracting gestures and unmotivated movements?

    _____

    _____

    _____

4. *Interpretation:* Did speaker place characters accurately and change smoothly from one character to another? Did speaker seem to understand the selection and accurately interpret the mood of the selection?

    _____

    _____

    _____

5. *Overall Comments*

    _____

    _____

    _____

Chapter 18
Group Interpretation

18.1 Define It

The Key Terms in Chapter 18 refer to performing oral interpretation in groups. Read the clues below. Then unscramble the letters and write the terms in the blanks.

Key Terms

choral speaking   script patterns
offstage focus   suggestion
reader's theatre

1. Directing one's eyes to the imagined reflection of other performers
    s c o f f g a t e o f u s
    _____

2. Type of group interpretation that involves speaking in unison
    g i n k p e a s a c h r o l
    _____

3. Ways in which speakers' parts are divided in group interpretation
    c i t a p r e s p r n t t s
    _____

4. Way in which reader's theatre performers create most of the action, props, and scenery in the audience's imagination
    g t o n s i e g u s
    _____

5. Type of group interpretation in which speakers present literature in a dramatic form
    e r a d t h r e e s r e t a
    _____

18.2 Variations on a Theme

The following poem was written by a junior-high-school student and published in a book created by her school. Using this poem, or one you or another student at your school has written, prepare two scripts. In groups of three or four students, decide on two different ways to perform the poem. Identify which voice(s) should read each line, and write the voice numbers in the lines next to the poem. Then present both versions to the class. Use audience feedback to decide which version is most effective.

Version 1 Voices	Society's Hazards	Version 2 Voices
_____	Tow away zone.	_____
_____	No parking at	_____
_____	Any time.	_____
_____	Fines.	_____
_____	Busses only,	_____
_____	Cars will be	_____
_____	Impounded.	_____
_____	No skating	_____
_____	On the sidewalk.	_____
_____	Dangerous waters.	_____
_____	Strong undertow.	_____
_____	Slippery when	_____
_____	Wet.	_____
_____	Caution.	_____
_____	Wet paint.	_____
_____	No soliciting of any kind.	_____

—Kristen Shrewsbury

Which version was most effective? _____

Describe why this version worked better than the other. _____

_____

18.3 Evaluating Choral Speaking

Listen to a choral-speaking performance. Write your comments and evaluate the group's overall performance.

Title of Selection _____

Group Members _____

Voice	**Always**	**Sometimes**	**Never**
Members' voices blended in unison	_____	_____	_____
Members started and stopped together.	_____	_____	_____
Members pronounced words in same way.	_____	_____	_____
Members varied vocal tone to show meaning.	_____	_____	_____
Body			
Members adapted facial expression to material.	_____	_____	_____
Members moved in unison.	_____	_____	_____
Members looked at listeners regularly	_____	_____	_____
Members entered and exited in unison.	_____	_____	_____
Scripts (if used)			
Members held scripts in similar ways.	_____	_____	_____
Member's faces could be seen over scripts.	_____	_____	_____
Material/Script Patterns			
The material was appropriate to the audience.	_____	_____	_____
The choice of script pattern helped communicate the meaning.	_____	_____	_____

Comments

_____

_____

_____

_____

_____

18.4 The Dramatic Athlete

Select an article from the sports pages of your local newspaper or school paper that contains vivid descriptions of a game. In groups of three to five students, develop the action paragraphs into short reader's theatre pieces and perform them for the class. Write one of your reader's theatre pieces in the space below. Indicate which voices will perform which lines.

Example

VOICE 1: Hawks thump Stars again.

VOICE 3: The Blackhawks and the Minnesota North Stars play bumper hockey the way kids play bumper cars.

VOICE 4: Even when time isn't running on the clock,

VOICE 1: these teams like to run into each other and

ALL: BOP

VOICE 1: each other

VOICE 2: just for fun

VOICE 3: in a personal game of

ALL: DARE-YOU-TO-CROSS-THIS-LINE!

VOICE 1

AND 2: Orneriness rules on nasty night.

ALL: Hawks thump Stars again.

Hawks thump Stars again
Orneriness rules on nasty night

The Blackhawks and the Minnesota North Stars play bumper hockey the way kids play bumper cars.

Even when time isn't running on the clock, these teams like to run into each other and bop each other just for fun in a personal game of dare-you-to-cross-this-line.

_____

_____

_____

_____

_____

_____

_____

_____

_____

18.5 Put It in Writing

Write a set of "Twelve Commandments for…" (parents, teachers, teens, younger siblings). Combine some or all of your commandments with those of three or four of your classmates. As a small group, decide how you might perform these commandments for the class using voices, movement, pantomime, and simple props.

> **Example**
> *Sample Commandments for Parents*
> 1. Thou shalt drive the car pool to the ends of the earth.
> 2. Thou shalt smile through a million recitals, plays, and ball games.
> 3. Thou shalt serve three dinners at twenty-minute intervals for busy teenagers.

Your Commandments

1. _____
2. _____
3. _____
4. _____
5. _____
6. _____
7. _____
8. _____
9. _____
10. _____
11. _____
12. _____

Performance Ideas

_____

_____

_____

_____

_____

18.6 Evaluating Group Reader's Theatre

Observe a reader's theatre performance that uses staging techniques.
Evaluate the overall effect of the performance by writing your responses in
each appropriate category.

Title of Selection _____

Group Members _____

Voice	**Always**	**Sometimes**	**Never**
Members blended in unison when appropriate.	_____	_____	_____
Voices could be distinguished from each other easily.	_____	_____	_____
Character voices remained the same throughout performance.	_____	_____	_____
Members used stress, pause, inflection, pitch, volume effectively.	_____	_____	_____
Body			
Members adapted facial expression to material.	_____	_____	_____
Members moved in unison when appropriate.	_____	_____	_____
Members looked at listeners regularly.	_____	_____	_____
Members entered and exited in unison.	_____	_____	_____
Scripts (if needed)			
Members held scripts in similar ways.	_____	_____	_____
Members' faces could be seen over scripts.	_____	_____	_____
Material			
Material was suitable to audience.	_____	_____	_____
Material was well scripted to show meaning.	_____	_____	_____
Material was suited to reader's theatre.	_____	_____	_____
Theme was communicated clearly.	_____	_____	_____

continued

18.6 Evaluating Group Reader's Theatre (continued)

Staging	Always	Sometimes	Never
Costumes, props, lights supported theme.	_____	_____	_____
Characters were consistently placed in back by speakers.	_____	_____	_____
Staging held interest of audience.	_____	_____	_____

Comments

_____

_____

_____

_____

_____

_____

_____

_____

_____

_____

_____

_____

_____

_____

_____

_____

_____

_____

_____

_____

_____